MERLEAU-PONTY'S LAST VISION

Northwestern University
Studies in Phenomenology
and
Existential Philosophy

MERLEAU-PONTY'S LAST VISION

A Proposal for the Completion of *The Visible and the Invisible*

Douglas Low

Northwestern University Press
Evanston, Illinois

Northwestern University Press
Evanston, Illinois 60208-4210

Printed in the United States of America

ISBN 0-8101-1806-8 (cloth)
ISBN 0-8101-1807-6 (paper)

Library of Congress Cataloging-in-Publication Data

Low, Douglas Beck, 1946–
Merleau-Ponty's last vision : a proposal for the completion of the visible and the invisible / Douglas Low.
p. cm.—(Northwestern University studies in phenomenology and existential philosophy)
Includes bibliographical references and index.
ISBN 0-8101-1806-8 (alk. paper)—ISBN 0-8101-1807-6 (pbk. : alk. paper)
1. Merleau-Ponty, Maurice, 1908–1961. Visible et l'invisible. 2. Ontology. 3. Knowledge, Theory of. I. Title. II. Series: Studies in phenomenology and existential philosophy.
B2430.M3763V5735 2000
111—dc21 00-008842

The paper used in this publication meets the minimum requirements of the American National Standard for Information Sciences—Permanence of Paper for Printed Library Materials, ANSI Z39.48-1984.

Dedicated to the memory of Maurice Merleau-Ponty

Contents

Preface xi

Acknowledgments xiii

Abbreviations xv

Introduction: A Proposal for Completing Merleau-Ponty's *The Visible and the Invisible* 1

Part 1. "The Visible and Nature"

1 Philosophical Interrogation 9

2 The Visible 29

3 Nature 38

4 Classical Ontology and Modern Ontology 56

Part 2. "The Invisible and *Logos*"

5 "The Invisible and *Logos*" 71

Notes 113

Bibliography 117

Index 121

Preface

The main goal of *Merleau-Ponty's Last Vision* is the attempted completion of the author's incomplete *The Visible and the Invisible* (*Le Visible et l'invisible,* 1964).[1] This is done by filling in Merleau-Ponty's 1960 outline for the text with his late essays (those that appear from 1952 onward) and his published lecture summaries from the Collège de France (which date from 1952 to 1960).

There are a number of reasons why I am undertaking this "dangerous" task of attempting to complete another author's work. First, the stature of the author and the importance of his ideas certainly warrant such an attempt. Second, Merleau-Ponty's works offer a valuable alternative to both modernism and postmodernism by coming between these positions and avoiding their untenable extremes. And third, the attempt should help determine more clearly the nature of Merleau-Ponty's *later* philosophy—which he was in the process of unfolding when he died in 1961. It is now well known that Merleau-Ponty's later works (1952–61) focus great attention on language, so much so that some have been led to claim that Merleau-Ponty abandons phenomenology and perception for a more postmodernist philosophy of language.[2] While I do not believe that Merleau-Ponty abandons phenomenology, he certainly does make greater room for language in his later philosophy of perception.[3] My purpose here is not to enter into a detailed polemic with differing interpretations of Merleau-Ponty's later works. I have made some attempt to do this elsewhere.[4] Throughout this text, however, I do interpret Merleau-Ponty's later works as coming between modernism and postmodernism.[5] Since *The Visible and the Invisible* is in such rough and incomplete form, and since there is such controversy about how this and other late texts of Merleau-Ponty's are to be interpreted,[6] I will often quote these texts at length. I do this to allow the texts to speak for themselves as much as possible. Now, I am fully aware that every exposition is an interpretation, and I believe that Merleau-Ponty was surely aware of this as well. And yet, just as surely he would have agreed that some interpretations are better than others. Some readings interpret more accurately and some are closer to the text as a whole. While I do not claim to here offer *the* interpretation, which would indeed be impossible, this work does try to confront and analyze these later texts on their own terms, in their proper context, and in their entirety. It is therefore to fulfill the goal of an accurate interpretation that the actual texts will be carefully analyzed and inspected, sometimes at length. It is to fulfill the goal of bringing these remarkable texts to greater public awareness that this "dangerous" task of completion has been undertaken.

Acknowledgments

I must first acknowledge and thank my close friends and colleagues: Joanne Hendricks, Scott and Susan Fisher, and Aziz Bettayeb—who have patiently listened to me and participated in many hours of discussion about the intricacies of Merleau-Ponty's philosophy. There can be no doubt, as Merleau-Ponty says, that the intellectual and psychological self is formed in social interaction. Even though I alone am ultimately responsible for what appears here, what does appear could not have been accomplished without the help and encouragement of these friends.

I am also grateful to the editors of Northwestern University Press for the many valuable suggestions that have resulted in a much improved text.

In addition, I would like to thank the members of the Merleau-Ponty Circle for their many stimulating presentations and their always friendly and collegial discussions. I am likewise grateful to Urbana University of Ohio for financing numerous trips to the Circle's annual conference.

And finally, a special thanks must be offered to Martha Banner and Peggy Kessler for their many hours of scrupulous work preparing the manuscript. Their editorial and computer skills, and the good-natured manner with which they exercise them, have made the preparation of the manuscript a social pleasure rather than an uncomfortable chore.

Abbreviations

Works by Merleau-Ponty cited frequently have been identified by the following abbreviations:

IPP	*In Praise of Philosophy,* 1963. *Eloge de la philosophie,* 1953.
PhP	*Phenomenology of Perception,* 1962; sixth printing, 1974, which includes translation corrections. *Phénoménologie de la perception,* 1945.
"PS"	"The Philosopher and Sociology," in *Signs,* 1964. *Signes,* 1960.
PrP	*The Primacy of Perception and Other Essays,* 1964. "Le Primat de la perception et ses conséquences philosophiques," 1946.
PW	*The Prose of the World,* 1973. *La Prose du monde,* 1969.
SB	*The Structure of Behavior,* 1963. *La Structure du comportement,* 1942.
TFL	*Themes from the Lectures at the Collège de France, 1952–1960,* 1970. *Résumés des cours, Collège de France, 1952–1960,* 1968.
VI	*The Visible and the Invisible,* 1968. *Le Visible et l'invisible,* 1964.

Introduction

A Proposal for Completing Merleau-Ponty's *The Visible and the Invisible*

> [A text] was sent to me [in 1952] by Merleau-Ponty at the time of his candidacy to the Collège de France, when I was putting together a report of his qualifications for presentation to the assembly of professors. In this report Merleau-Ponty traces his past and future as a philosopher in a continuous line, and outlines the perspectives of his future studies from *L'Origine de la vérite* [retitled *Le Visible et l'invisible*] to *L'Homme transcendental.* In reading these unpublished and highly interesting pages, one keenly regrets the death which brutally interrupted the élan of a profound thought in full possession of itself and about to fulfill itself in a series of original works which would have been landmarks in contemporary French philosophy.
>
> —*Martial Gueroult*

Maurice Merleau-Ponty must certainly be placed among the greatest of France's twentieth-century philosophers. He is perhaps even its greatest. At the time of his appointment to the Collège de France, at just forty-four years of age, he was the youngest member ever to be elected to the faculty of this most prestigious research institution. Just nine years after his appointment, his totally unexpected death in 1961, at the relatively young age of fifty-three, sent a shock of regret and loss through the intellectual world. The loss of this first-rate and original thinker was felt all the more keenly because it interrupted an original text that seemed to be fully conceived yet not fully delivered. This partially completed text was published posthumously in 1964, under the editorship of Claude Lefort, along with some working notes, under the full title *Le Visible et l'invisible: suivi de notes de travail.*[1] Its English translation, *The Visible and the Invisible: Followed by Working Notes* (herein abbreviated as *VI*), appeared just four years later in 1968. Judging from an outline[2] of the proposed text written by Merleau-Ponty (probably in November or December of 1960),[3] he had completed in rough form approximately the first one-fourth of part 1. This November/December outline appears to be the last complete outline written by Merleau-Ponty, though several preceded it (see *VI* xxxv–xxxvi), and one abbreviated outline written in March 1961 succeeds it (see *VI* 274). Here is the March 1961 outline:

I. The Visible
II. Nature
III. Logos

The March 1961 outline is the last entry of the working notes published in *The Visible and the Invisible* and must surely be one of the last passages written by Merleau-Ponty before his untimely death on May 3 of the same year. It is followed by a few brief comments, and it is much more briefly stated than the November/December 1960 outline. Even though there are minor differences between the two outlines, mostly in the placement of headings, they do not differ in any substantial way. Here is the November/December 1960 outline:

I. The Visible and Nature
Philosophical Interrogation
interrogation and reflection;
interrogation and dialectic;
interrogation and intuition
The Visible
Nature
Classical Ontology and Modern Ontology
II. The Invisible and *Logos*

And here is the table of contents of the roughly completed chapters of *The Visible and the Invisible,* as edited and presented by Claude Lefort:

The Visible and Invisible: Philosophical Interrogation
1. Reflection and Interrogation
2. Interrogation and Dialectic
3. Interrogation and Intuition
4. The Intertwining—the Chiasm

The first three chapters directly above obviously complete, or at least write out in rough form, the first section of part 1 of the November/

December 1960 outline, the section entitled "Philosophical Interrogation," for the section and chapter headings match almost exactly. It might also be argued, but with less certainty and a greater degree of speculation, that chapter 4, "The Intertwining—the Chiasm," because its content focuses in part on bodily perception, begins to fill out the second section, "The Visible," of part 1 of the November/December 1960 outline.

Regrettably, these four chapters are all we have that were actually completed by the author, along with approximately one hundred pages of highly informative notes.[4] However, we can also examine a collection of Merleau-Ponty's lecture summaries, written by the author himself and published as *Themes from the Lectures at the Collège de France, 1952–1960* (*Résumés des cours, Collège de France, 1952–1960*).[5] These are lecture summaries that he prepared and delivered during or just before the years when he was composing *The Visible and the Invisible* (his notes for this manuscript date from January 1959 to March 1961). We find that these lectures display titles that in many cases match or fit under the titles of the November/December 1960 outline of *The Visible and the Invisible.* Thus, a means has perhaps been found to fill in the 1960 outline more completely, for the 1952–60 matching lectures give us a much more complete idea of what the outlined sections would have looked like. Using *Themes from the Lectures* (*TFL*) to complete *The Visible and the Invisible* obviously involves at least a degree of speculation, for Merleau-Ponty's thought was continually developing and unfolding from 1952 to the time of his death in 1961. Perhaps these lectures lead up to thoughts that significantly supersede those that preceded them. This certainly must be kept in mind. However, since the two time periods are so close and in fact overlap (*TFL* 1952–60; *VI* notes 1959–61), and since the lecture titles match the outline's section headings so well, there is ample reason to believe that the content of these two works overlaps as well. Moreover, this reasoning is confirmed by reference to the comments made by Claude Lefort, who was a close friend of Merleau-Ponty's and his posthumous editor. After Merleau-Ponty's death, he edited and brought to print *The Prose of the World* (*La Prose du monde,* 1969)[6] as well as the already mentioned *The Visible and the Invisible.* In the editor's preface to *The Prose of the World* (*PW*), he calculates that the manuscript for it was probably written in 1951 (*PW* xiv—xv) and that it was abandoned by the author in the fall or winter of that year (*PW* xiv). However, he goes on to make the following claim:

> [A reader familiar with Merleau-Ponty's *The Visible and the Invisible*] will see, in *The Prose of the World,* a new conception appear of man's relation with history and with truth; he will discover, in the meditation on "indirect language," the first signs of the "indirect ontology" which sustains *The Visible and the Invisible.* If he rereads the notes of the latter, moreover, he will

> see that questions raised in the earlier manuscript [*The Prose of the World*] are reformulated in many places and in similar terms, and—whether involving language, structure, history, or literary creation—are intended to be included in the work in progress. We therefore unhesitantly respond negatively to the question, does the abandonment of the manuscript constitute a disavowal? The very term "abandonment" seems to us equivocal. "Abandonment" implies that Merleau-Ponty would never have returned to the work he had started with the sole intention of giving it a finish that it lacked. On the other hand, it must be admitted that *The Prose of the World,* down to the very literalness of certain analyses, could have been reborn in the tissue of *The Visible and the Invisible,* if the latter had not itself been interrupted by the philosopher's death. (*PW* xix–xx)

If Lefort is right about the reintegration of *The Prose of the World* into *The Visible and the Invisible,* and I believe he is, it can be claimed a fortiori that *Themes from the Lectures* would have undergone a similar reintegration, for it extends the themes mentioned in *The Prose of the World,* particularly with regard to language,[7] and is even closer in time to the composition of *The Visible and the Invisible.* Obviously one must read *Themes from the Lectures* as building up to *The Visible and the Invisible.* Yet because of the closeness in time, the similarity of content, and the matching title headings, there is ample reason to believe that *Themes from the Lectures* would have been integrated into *The Visible and the Invisible.* It must be remembered, as Lefort remarks with respect to *The Prose of the World,*[8] that this integration would surely have changed the earlier works. But again, because they are so close in time, content, and subject headings, if we consider them carefully, at least some insight can be gained into what the unfinished *The Visible and the Invisible* would have looked like if it had been completed.

Since much may potentially be gained by using *Themes from the Lectures* to get a more complete picture of the unfinished *The Visible and the Invisible,* it is reasonable to propose that *Themes from the Lectures* be used as proxy (as an imperfect and incomplete substitute) for the sections that Merleau-Ponty outlined in November/December 1960. It is also reasonable to propose that several other works actually published by Merleau-Ponty during this last period of his life (1952–61) be used to help complete *The Visible and the Invisible*—at least in general terms. One of the main themes of Merleau-Ponty's late essay "Eye and Mind" ("L'Oeil et l'esprit," 1961)[9] is overcoming and providing an alternative to Descartes's classical ontology. Adopting the terminology of art history, Merleau-Ponty refers to the Cartesian coordinate system in ontology and the geometrical (linear) perspective in painting as "classical" and to the forms of thought and painting that began to break with them as "modern." (In the terminology of contemporary philosophy, the former would be referred to as "modern" and the latter as "postmodern.") The terminology and content of "Eye and Mind" thus perfectly matches the terminology of the section entitled "Classical Ontology and Modern Ontology" in the November/December 1960 outline for *The Visible and the Invisible.* The essay first appeared in the inaugural issue of *Art de France* in January 1961 and is thus of the same period as *The Visible and the Invisible.* Thus, based on both content and date of appearance, it is reasonable to assume that the essay's main ideas would have been incorporated in *The Visible and the Invisible* under the section heading of "Classical Ontology and Modern Ontology." ("Eye and Mind" is now one of the essays collected in *The Primacy of Perception* [*PrP*], 1964.)

In another example of this process, Merleau-Ponty's article "Indirect Language and the Voices of Silence" ("Le Langage indirect et les voix du Silence," 1952) first appeared as a chapter in his unfinished manuscript *The Prose of the World.* (See Lefort's *PW* preface, xx.) After being greatly revised and rewritten, it was first published in 1952 in *Les Temps Modernes* (*PW* xiv) and was later republished in Merleau-Ponty's book *Signs* (*Signes,* 1960).[10] Another 1952 article on language, entitled "On the Phenomenology of Language" ("Sur la phénoménologie du langage," 1952), was also republished in *Signes* in 1960. The fact that Merleau-Ponty republishes both works in 1960, without changes, indicates that he still accepts their main themes, which undoubtedly would have been incorporated into *The Visible and the Invisible* (begun in 1959) under the heading of "The Invisible and *Logos.*"

Here, then, is the proposal for helping Merleau-Ponty complete *The Visible and the Invisible* using his own published lectures and articles to fill in the 1960 outline. The suggested additions to the 1960 outline are placed in brackets followed by the text in which they appear. Merleau-Ponty's section and chapter headings have also been numbered.

Part I. The Visible and Nature

Section I. Philosophical Interrogation

1. Interrogation and Reflection
2. Interrogation and Dialectic
3. Interrogation and Intuition[11]

Section II. The Visible

4. The Intertwining—the Chiasm

Section III. Nature

[The Concept of Nature I, *TFL*]

[The Concept of Nature II: Animality, the Human Body, Transition to Culture, *TFL*]

[Nature and Logos: The Human Body, *TFL*]
Section IV. Classical Ontology and Modern Ontology
["Eye and Mind," *PrP*]
Part II. The Invisible and *Logos*
Section V. The Invisible and *Logos*
[The Sensible World and the World of Expression, *TFL*]
[Studies in the Literary Use of Language, *TFL*]
[The Problem of Speech, *TFL*]
[Institution in Personal and Public History, *TFL*]
[The Problem of Passivity: Sleep, the Unconscious, Memory, *TFL*]
[Husserl at the Limits of Phenomenology, *TFL*]
["On the Phenomenology of Language," *Signs*]
["Indirect Language and the Voices of Silence," *Signs*]

As was noted briefly above, the placement of chapter 4, "The Intertwining—the Chiasm," is perhaps the most speculative element of the current proposal, but, as was also mentioned above, this chapter is brought under the heading of "The Visible" because the main focus of the chiasm chapter is the chiasm (intersection, or crisscrossing) between the human body and the world that produces perceptual meaning, i.e., the visible or sensible.

Moreover, an additional word is perhaps needed to justify the lecture and essay titles here brought under the heading "The Invisible and *Logos*," which composes part 2 of the outline. Broadly speaking, the *invisible* for Merleau-Ponty refers to ideas and *logos* refers to speech, to the sense that is found in the human body's active interaction with the world and with others and that is prolonged and sublimated by speech to create abstract ideas. All the lectures or articles listed under part 2 were written after 1952, and are thus close to or overlap with the composition of *The Visible and the Invisible.* They all deal with expression, speech, and language.[12]

Of course, completing another author's work is a highly risky and speculative task, even when using the author's own works and words to do so. However, this risk is perhaps worth it, for at least it helps to close the last chapter of Merleau-Ponty's tragically short life, to bring some sort of emotional closure to those who still feel deprived of his genius by his sudden and unexpected death. Yet even more than the emotional closure, it helps us reconstruct the last work of a highly original mind, to get at least some more detailed idea of what this last work may have looked like. Merleau-Ponty's ideas remain vitally relevant today. The more we can clarify the ideas that were "brutally interrupted," the greater will be their contribution.

PART 1

"THE VISIBLE AND NATURE"

1

Philosophical Interrogation

Interrogation . . . and Reflection, Dialectic, Intuition

In November 1991 an international conference took as its theme the question of the relevance of Merleau-Ponty's philosophy to current philosophical issues and debates.[1] The participants focused on Merleau-Ponty's last and posthumously published text, *The Visible and the Invisible.* The answer to their question (it seems without exception) was that his works do remain relevant—even vitally so. With this in mind, I will present what I believe are the main themes of *The Visible and the Invisible,* differing in some cases with the interpretations offered at the above-mentioned conference. Where and when I can, I will try to point out some of the relevance of Merleau-Ponty's last text for contemporary philosophy. I will also pay close attention to the arguments that Merleau-Ponty gives to establish his position.

Among the main themes of the last text must certainly be counted Merleau-Ponty's attempt to get at the meaning of Being—including the meaning of seeing and knowing, the meaning of self, consciousness, and language. What Merleau-Ponty says of Heidegger's philosophy could be said of his own last philosophical attempt:

> It is beyond such correlatives [of Being and Nothingness] . . . that philosophy takes it start, namely, in the "there exists," in an "opening" toward "something," toward "that which is not nothing." It is this preobjective Being, between the inert essences or *quidditas* and the individual localized at a point in space-time, that is the proper theme of philosophy. (*TFL* 110)

Merleau-Ponty's last philosophy is concerned primarily with making sense of "there exists," of the existence of the world as it appears before us.

The opening passage of *The Visible and the Invisible* makes this clear:

> We see the things themselves, the world is what we see: formulae of this kind express a faith common to the natural man and the philosopher—the moment he opens his eyes: they refer to a deep-seated set of mute "opinions" implicated in our lives. But what is strange about this faith is that if we seek to articulate it into theses or statements, if we ask ourselves what is this *we,* what *seeing* is, what *thing* or *world* is, we enter into a labyrinth of difficulties and contradictions.
>
> What Saint Augustine said of time—that it is perfectly familiar to each, but that none of us can explain it to the others—must be said of the world. (*VI* 3)

According to Merleau-Ponty's analysis, then, at the level of perception human beings live in the world. It is there. We have a faith that we are reaching it. We even have the experience of reaching it where it rests but also, and simultaneously, that it appears at the end of our gaze, and therefore only in our minds, or at least in our bodies. Thus, if we try to articulate our perceptual faith, we immerse ourselves in difficulties and contradictions. Yet the bringing of this perceptual contact with the world to expression is what the philosopher must attempt to do. (Moreover, this faith is not the faith of religion, which is the acceptance of something that is not seen. Nor is it the faith of a judgment, a decision made. It is the acceptance of the world's givenness in lived-through perception. It is perceptual faith, an animal faith that is prior to any abstract, intellectual thesis [*VI* 3, note]).

After this initial claim of his intent, Merleau-Ponty turns quickly to an analysis of skepticism, particularly with regard to perception. He investigates the claim that supposedly veridical perception *could be* a dream, an illusion, or a hallucination. These arguments claim that because any *particular* perception could be called into question, because no *particular* perception is given with certainty, that perception in *general* is unreliable and must therefore be called into question.

Merleau-Ponty answers this skepticism with some forceful arguments of his own. First, he points out that these skeptical arguments always presuppose the acceptance of a second or subsequent perception that calls the first into question. The only way one perception is challenged as false is from the point of view of another that has been accepted as true. Furthermore, when a dream or an illusion displaces the world, is taken to be more real than the world, this dream borrows the sense of existence from the world (where else would it come from) without realizing that it does so or without elucidating its own meaning of existence. If the dream did not assume its own givenness and questioned the meaning of its own existence, the whole process of doubt would begin again and leave us with nothing, not even the dream or the illusion. Merleau-Ponty escapes this misguided nihilism by not first doubting the world's existence. He seeks rather to elucidate its meaning. Since it is already within experience, he seeks to elucidate what is there. He seeks to discover "what it is for it to exist" (*VI* 96).

Second, Merleau-Ponty points out that these skeptical arguments presuppose that we already have some idea of the *thing in itself* that we are not reaching, a pure thing in itself that is set against our "interior life." Merleau-Ponty responds by saying that we must not make this assumption, that we must try to describe how these meanings come about within us, how perceived thing, imagined thing, and so on come about within us. "We have to reformulate the skeptical arguments outside of every ontological preconception and reformulate them precisely as to know what world-being, thing-being, imaginary being, and conscious being are" (*VI* 6–7).

Here we have Merleau-Ponty explicitly taking up the ontological questions: what is it for the world, a thing, a consciousness, and language to exist? Moreover, how is it that my gaze seems to reach the thing itself, where it rests, and yet that it appears only at the end of my gaze and therefore occurs within me? The answers to these questions constitute the main themes of *The Visible and the Invisible:* (1) the meaning of Being (including that of world, thing, consciousness, and language); (2) the resolution of the paradox of "how is it that I perceive the things themselves, where they rest, and that they occur within me, on this side of my body?"; and (3) the expression of perceptual faith (of reaching the world where it rests) in a positive thesis.

Turning from the analysis of skepticism, Merleau-Ponty goes on to give a more positive description of experience: If I start with lived experience and seek to describe it without any of the presuppositions of skepticism, I must acknowledge "that the thing is at the end of my gaze." "I must acknowledge that the table before me sustains a singular relation with my eyes and my body. I see it only if it is within their radius of action" (*VI* 7). In addition, because the movement of my body influences my perception, I must acknowledge a "subjective" or "corporeal component" to experience (*VI* 8). Thus, even within the context of this first attempt at a presuppositionless description of experience, we are still left with the same above-stated paradox.

Perhaps, however, if I turn from my own direct experience to what others can offer, to what others experience of me, I will resolve these problems. Unfortunately "the other men who see as we do . . . present us with but an amplification of the same paradox" (*VI* 9), for I perceive another *human* presence, yet again with no real access to the other, who seems to be only a projection of my own. Yet, Merleau-Ponty continues, the other's life *does* break through my private life, and even though I know that the other life may simply be my projection, "my private world has ceased to be mine only; it is now the instrument which another plays, the dimension of a generalized life which is grafted onto my own" (*VI* 11). On the other hand, "at the moment that I think I share the life of another, I am rejoining it only in its ends, its exterior poles. It is in the world that we communicate" (*VI* 11). "It is from this lawn before me that I think I catch sight of the impact of the green on the vision of another" (*VI* 11). We do *live* this communication with others, "yet we can neither think it nor formulate it nor set it up in thesis" (*VI* 11). Thus, even within the description of direct experience, with a consideration of the other, and without the presuppositions of skepticism and classical philosophy, we are still left with the same problems.

In a subsequent section on science and perceptual faith, Merleau-Ponty asks the following question. Does not science with its claims to an objective truth established by measurement and the functional operations of algorithms resolve the problems of lived experience? His answer is no, for ever since the problems introduced by scale (at the microscopic and macroscopic levels), which imply the involvement of the perceiver, "we have seen many physicists seek . . . arguments in favor of determinism, or, contrariwise, of a 'mental' or 'acausal' reality. These alternatives show enough to what point science . . . is rooted in pre-science and foreign to the question of the *meaning of being*" (*VI* 16). Furthermore, human perception cannot be explained by an objective causality. The elements of our gestalt perceptual field cannot be calculated mathematically or objectively, for the horizon or background participates with the foreground in a way that is meaningful to the perceiver but that cannot be ideally calculated.

In his criticism of science, Merleau-Ponty of course does not claim that perception can occur without the body. Rather he claims that we must rethink the body and its relationship to the world—going beyond the objective body of science, with its distinct parts placed in external, mechanical, or functional relationships to one another. For Merleau-Ponty, the human body is between a thing in itself and a being for itself, between pure thing and pure consciousness. It is a third kind of thing. It is like a thing because it has thickness and opaqueness, yet it is the thing that is conscious, that opens out unto the world. Since its parts fit together like a gestalt whole, since they are organized meaningfully, and since consciousness is a relation to the world, the perceived thing is organized like the body, that is, meaningfully, like the elements of a gestalt whole. This rethinking of the body and its lived-through perceptual relationship to the world puts it at odds with the scientifically conceived body as a thing with discrete parts in external relationship to each other and with the body conceived from the point of view of a disembodied knower.

Merleau-Ponty's purpose here is not to reject science and "objective knowledge" and to oppose to it a realm of "subjective truths," but, he says, to show that these classical alternatives rest on a lived perception which lies beneath their separation.

In a section dealing with perceptual faith and reflection, Merleau-Ponty states that since science alone cannot resolve our difficulties, philosophy must still seek to understand our openness unto the world as well as how the world is hidden from us—and how these occur together. It cannot do so simply by vacillating between the one and the other, between my vision reaching the things and my vision occurring in me. The philosopher must *reflect* in order to try to understand this discord at a deeper level. Once this is done, "a third dimension seems to open up, wherein their discordance is effaced. With the conversion to reflection, perceiving and imagining are now only two modes of *thinking*. From vision and feeling will be retained only what animates them and sustains them indubitably, pure thought of seeing or of feeling" (*VI* 28–29).

While Merleau-Ponty sees reflection as an essential step in the quest for truth, he sees a serious problem with the philosophy of reflection that seeks to constitute the world intellectually. The problem is that it does not reflect on its own role. It is not radical enough. The philosophy of reflection traces the constitution of the world and its objects back to their intellectual source. But then this tracing backward is not the same as the forward constitution. Reconstruction does not mirror the original constitution, since it moves in the opposite direction. Reflection and reflective constitution therefore do not account for what they may add. They do not account for their own role (*VI* 33).

Furthermore, reflection by its very nature is *re*-flective. It comes second and looks back at something more primary (*VI* 34). And even though idealist reflection continues to draw on the prereflective, idealist philosophers give a typical response to save their position. Merleau-Ponty characterizes the response in this way:

> The [idealist] reply will perhaps be . . . that one begins with the unreflected, because one does have to begin, but the universe of thought that is opened up by a reflection contains everything necessary to account

> for the mutilated thought of the beginning, which is only the ladder one pulls up after oneself after having climbed it. (*VI* 34–35)

Merleau-Ponty goes on to answer this attempted rescue of idealism as follows:

> But if [the above-stated idealist claim] is so, there is no longer any philosophy of reflection, for there is no longer the originating and the derived; there is a thought traveling a circle where the condition and the conditioned, the reflection and the unreflected, are in a reciprocal, if not symmetrical, relationship, and where the end is in the beginning as much as the beginning is in the end. (*VI* 35)

After registering this criticism of idealism Merleau-Ponty goes on to immediately state his own position:

> We are not saying anything different. The remarks we made concerning reflection were nowise intended to disqualify it for the profit of the unreflected or the immediate (which we know only through reflection). It is a question not of putting the perceptual faith in place of reflection, but on the contrary of taking into account the total situation, which involves reference from the one to the other. What is given is not a massive and opaque world, or a universe of adequate thought; it is a reflection which turns back over the density of the world in order to clarify it, but which, coming second, reflects back to it only its own light. (*VI* 35)

For Merleau-Ponty, then, the relationship between *noesis* and *noema,* between an act of thinking and its object, does not capture our relationship to the world. It certainly does not capture the richness of our *entire* relationship to the world, nor does it capture even our essential relationship to it. Thinking and its relationship to the world as thought rests upon and presupposes our lived encounter with the world. It is to this lived encounter that both thought and reflection *return* as already present.

What we must do, as Merleau-Ponty says in *Phenomenology of Perception* (*Phénoménologie de la perception,* 1945) and repeats in a different language here, is step back, loosen our bonds with the world, that is, *reflect,* and *watch* the meanings that are formed in the body's lived encounter with the world fly up like sparks from a fire.[2] In thus reflecting upon experience, one of the meanings discovered is that the distinction between the real and the imaginary is given there in the experiences themselves. When reflecting on experience we see that the most vivid image breaks up with the least interruption or inspection, and, conversely, even the weakest noise is read as an index to reality. "This simple fact imposes upon us the idea that with the 'real' and the 'imaginary' we are dealing with two 'orders,' two 'stages,' or two 'theaters'—that of space and that of phantasms—which are set up within us before the acts of discrimination (which intervene only in the equivocal cases), and in which what we live comes to settle outside all criteriological control" (*VI* 39–40). Moreover, the experience of dis-illusion teaches us even more precisely *what* the real *is* and, in addition, *how fragile* it is. "For when an illusion dissipates, when an appearance suddenly breaks up, it is always for the profit of a new appearance which takes up again for its own account the ontological function of the first" (*VI* 40). Merleau-Ponty continues:

> What I can conclude from these disillusions or deceptions, therefore, is that perhaps 'reality' does not belong definitely to any particular perception, that in this sense it lies always further on; but this does not authorize me to break or to ignore the bond that joins them one after the other to the real, the bond that cannot be broken with one without having been established with the following. (*VI* 40–41)

We can therefore always call a particular perception into account; we can call it probable or even an opinion, but what we cannot doubt is the "same familiar Being" to which all perceptions, even if false, belong (*VI* 46). Thus, even though Merleau-Ponty argues that the world is given to us through human perception, the world runs beyond this perception. There is a transcendence of the world given in the immanence of experience. The world or Being phenomenalizes itself to us in perception, presents itself as existent through human perception. Perception does not cut the perceiver off from the world, as if the perceiver sees only a sense datum or quale. Perception is our very contact with the world's existence.

Merleau-Ponty adopts what has sometimes been called a disclosure theory of truth, that perceptions unfold and lead progressively to a more complete grasping of the thing perceived. Each perception, as we have seen, may be called into question or canceled, but only by others that are accepted, that replace it. Thus, there is a series of perceptions that are not merely appearances in the mind of a "for itself," but are an active opening of an incarnate consciousness upon a world of which it is a part. Perceptions, even those that may be false, are thus "radiations of this unique world that 'there is' " (*VI* 41). As Merleau-Ponty says:

> The movement toward adequation, to which the facts of dis-illusion bear witness, is not the returning to itself of an adequate thought that would have inexplicably lost sight of itself—nor is it blind progress of probability. . . . It is in the prepossession of a totality which is there before one knows how and why, whose realizations are never what we would have imagined them to be, and which nonetheless fulfills a secret explanation within us, since we believe in it tirelessly. (*VI* 42)

This statement moves us closer to Merleau-Ponty's resolution of the paradox of perception (that it reaches the things where they rest and yet that perception occurs on this side of the body). We are beginning to see that it is because perception is embodied, because the human body is in the world like other objects, that it has access to them. Yet it is also because the human body is different from the things, because it is the thing that gives access to other things, that it is separate from them. It is a separation that nevertheless carries us to the things themselves, as we shall see below.

So much of Merleau-Ponty's thought can be understood as an effort to come between traditional philosophy's alternatives of materialism/idealism, empiricism/rationalism, object/subject, and fact/essence. In a chapter concerned with the philosophies of reflection (Descartes and especially Kant and Husserl) and with the philosophy of coincidence (Bergson), Merleau-Ponty has some significant things to say about traditional philosophy's typical fact/essence distinction.

According to Merleau-Ponty, the philosophy of reflection does not doubt the existence of the world but seeks to discover the meaning existence has for us. It seeks the *essence* of what it is to exist. It seeks the necessary conditions for the existence of being. Yet, since the philosophy of reflection does not doubt the existence of the world, since it wants to discover what the existence of the world means for us, then there is something prior to reflection that reflection seeks to elucidate.

What is this prior knowledge? Does it define it well to say that it is essence? No, for the essence itself is dependent. Kant's famous refrain states: If the world is to exist, then certain conditions must necessarily be present. "But," Merleau-Ponty asks, "whence do we get the hypothesis . . . that there is a world?" There must be a prior knowledge beneath the essence that the essence relies upon but does not grasp (*VI* 109).

Furthermore, an essence does not give us Being (*Sein*). It gives us a particular manner of Being (*Sosein*). Essences do not give us the necessary conditions for all possible being. They give us particular ways of being. Moreover, Merleau-Ponty says, if essences do possess any universal value, it is because they make sense of an experience that is similar in human beings as they open upon a shared world, and not because they preexist in the mind, in nature, or in some realm of ideas (*VI* 109–10).

But, some might well object to Merleau-Ponty, you are using essences to express this claim. Yes, Merleau-Ponty admits. Yet, he goes on, "[essence] indeed only survives my own intuition of the moment and is valid for me as a durable truth because my own experience interconnects within itself and connects with that of others by opening upon one sole world" (*VI* 110). For Merleau-Ponty, consciousness is not a private awareness of one's own interior but a relation to the world. Consciousness is *ek-stace;* it is an active transcendence toward the world.[3] It is a field, *a spatial and temporal* field. Moreover, time itself is *ek-stace,* for the present is an active leaping out of itself toward the past and the future. Since consciousness fuses with temporality, consciousness (especially as perception) opens to a field (both spatial and temporal) that runs beyond it, that opens it to other temporalities, to the experiences of others, to other possibilities. This leads Merleau-Ponty to conclude the following:

> Every ideation, because it is an ideation, is formed in a space of existence, under the guarantee of my duration, which must turn back into itself in order to find there the same idea I thought an instant ago and must pass into the others in order to rejoin it also in them. Every ideation is borne by this tree of my duration and their durations . . . ; behind the idea, there is the unity, the simultaneity of all the real and possible durations, the cohesion of one sole Being from one end to the other. Under the solidity of the essence and of the idea, there is the fabric of experience, this flesh of time. (*VI* 111)

This is perhaps an opportune time to point out the fundamental difference between Merleau-Ponty's last philosophy of existence and Derrida's philosophy of deconstruction.[4] Within Merleau-Ponty's philosophy the immanent *awareness* of time (without which the moments of time would not *pass*) opens to and fuses with time as transcendent (a solely immanently constituted time would destroy time, for it is the nature of time to be *deployed* and not set out spatially before a constituting subject). The present moment of time is *ek-stace;* it transcends itself toward a past and a future that are other than it yet with which it remains in contact. It is Merleau-Ponty's thesis of the primacy of bodily perception that provides the basis for grasping the experience of time, for perception is *ek-stace,* a leaping out of oneself toward the world. Perception is dehiscence, a splitting open of the body as touching and touched, as seer and seen that allows the body to experience things, that puts the body in contact with things where they rest, yet that separates it from them at the same time.

The body's dehiscence helps it form a chiasm with things, a crisscrossing which is at the same time a contact and a separation. It is a dehiscence which throws the incarnate self out into a world that includes it and others, a lived world that acts as the ground for self, others, and the ideas shared between them.

Within Derrida's philosophy the immanence of a constantly deferring language (which, it appears, generates time and space) reaches no transcendent term. Derrida argues that there is difference because *différance* is a play of signifiers that refers only to other signifiers and not to a signified—be it a thing or a concept. There is no presence of the perceived to the perceiver or even of perception with itself, for the language which expresses these ideas is nothing but a deferring that leaves only a trace of connectedness between signifiers and therefore never a full presence of signifiers to each other or to the signified.

We may characterize the difference between the two above-stated philosophies as follows. For Merleau-Ponty, perception (as we have seen) and language (as we shall see) refer to something beyond them that acts as their open-ended support. For Derrida there is no perception and signifiers refer only to other signifiers. For Merleau-Ponty, language and ideas are carried by existence, by an incarnate opening upon a world that is really there for me and others. For Derrida, the load and what carries it are reversed, for now it is language that is the vehicle for everything else. It must also be noted here that Merleau-Ponty never accepts the full presence of self with perceived thing or of self with self that Derrida criticizes in Husserl. For Merleau-Ponty, there is never full coincidence with thing or self, since the body as perceiving and the body as perceived never coincide in the temporal flow of experience. Presence is always given in the context of spatial and temporal difference, a difference that is nevertheless held together by a transcendent world and by the human body that opens out unto it and partially fuses with it.

Merleau-Ponty states explicitly that it is this "fabric of experience," this "flesh of time" that allows us to connect with the world and others and yet also prevents us from penetrating "into the hard core of being":

> My incontestable power to give leeway, to disengage the possible from the real, does not go so far as to dominate all the implications of the spectacle and to make of the real a simple variant of the possible; on the contrary, it is the possible worlds and possible beings that are the variants and are like doubles of the actual world and actual Being. (*VI* 111–12)

These comments are undoubtedly aimed at reflective philosophies in general and at Husserl's eidetic reduction in particular (see *PrP* 68 ff.)[5]—

whereby the reflective subject begins with a concrete experience of a particular thing, and then varies this thing in the imagination to find its essential structure. Once this essence is discovered, it will then be used to fix the possibility of all the variations for this particular object. Thus, once the essence is defined, it provides the necessary conditions for the appearance of the particular object under consideration. Here essence determines existence and the possibility of existence. Here the real is a variant of the possible—which is determined by the essence. Merleau-Ponty, however, has just argued that the real is not a variant of the possible, but that it is the possible that is a variant of the real. By starting with a concrete experience of a concrete thing, we can reflect (we do have some leeway) in order to compare the object to other objects and to compare our experience to other experiences and the experiences that occur to other subjects. This allows us to determine the inessential, what does not belong to the essence of the object or experience. It does not allow us to determine the essential. To do this, the reflecting knower would have to be outside of all situatedness, outside of all time and space, outside one's own incarnate duration, which would be impossible, and which is the very thing that gives one access to the world and things and the possibility of forming at least an idea of the inessential.

One reason why essences have been traditionally separated from facts is the unwarranted assumption of a pure knower, a "*kosmotheoros*" confronting the particular things in their own specific place and time. Here "one is led to conceive another dimension that would be a transversal to this flat multiplicity and that would be the system of significations without locality or temporality" (*VI* 113). But am I a pure knower who grasps pure meanings in an invisible realm beyond space and time? No, for as soon as I grasp an essence, I realize that it soon drifts away from my *present* awareness, that the knower and the essences are themselves situated in time and in space. "The visible can thus fill me . . . only because I who see it do not see it from the depths of nothingness, but from the midst of itself" (*VI* 113). And this being the case, "facts and essences can no longer be distinguished . . . because . . . the alleged facts, the spatio-temporal individuals, are from the first mounted on the axes, the pivots, the dimensions, the generality of my body, and the ideas are therefore already encrusted in its joints" (*VI* 114). This claim leads to the following conclusion:

> We never have before us pure individuals, . . . nor essences without place and without date. Not that they exist elsewhere, beyond our grasp, but because we are experiences, that is, thoughts that feel behind themselves the weight of the space, the time, the very Being they think. (*VI* 115)

Within Merleau-Ponty's philosophy we thus find facts and essences given together in lived experience, in the body's lived encounter with the world. Moreover, since facts and essences are given together, we can reject the traditional and Husserlian separation of the intuition of essences (*wesenschau*) and induction. Intuition does not take us to a separate realm of meaning. At least initially, meaning is given in the body's concrete encounter with worldly things. True, abstraction helps release meaning from the prereflective, lived-through moment, but these meanings do not exist in a transtemporal and transpatial realm. As we have just seen, they are carried by the duration of my existence, a duration that opens me out to one sole being, a duration that expresses my encounter with the world and others. Furthermore, there is no pure inductivity. Rather than a straightforward generalization from sense particulars, we see experiences of a particular bearing a general meaning; we see experiences correcting each other; we see a dialogical or dialectical formation of general ideas. And finally:

> Along this route, at least, it is indeed certain that we gain access to objectivity, not by penetrating into an In Itself, but by disclosing, rectifying each by the other, the exterior datum and the internal double of it that we possess insofar as we are sensible-sentients, archetypes and variants of humanity and of life, that is, insofar as we are within life, within the human being and within Being, and insofar as it is in us as well, and insofar as we live and know not halfway between opaque facts and limpid ideas, but at the point of intersection and overlapping where families of facts inscribe their generality, their kinship, group themselves about the dimensions and the site of our own existence. (*VI* 116)

Within Merleau-Ponty's philosophy the essence and fact are given together in lived, incarnate experience, in the body's lived encounter with the world. Essence and fact are given actively as a verb and not as a fixed thing with its properties defined in isolation. Fact and essence are given actively because the *body* is active, yet also because the world and its things are active. First of all, the world is not like a single thing or even a sum of things; it is the ground of all things, that from which all things emerge. Second, the world and its things are given temporally, as processes, as structures unfolding in time—not as fixed individuals. (See *TFL* 91 ff.) Thus, nature itself (the world and its objects) should be treated more like a verb than a noun. Nature actively, temporally unfolds itself to an active subject, to an embodied subject that is a bit of matter, a bit of the world actively folding over on itself and the world, and thus revealing both.

We must remember, then, that for Merleau-Ponty the body is the proof of the existence of the world. My body is a thing like other things, *feels* their *existence* within it because it is one of them, and *more,* is *aware* of them, feels what it is like to exist as a thing from the *inside.* Nature thus becomes aware of itself through one of its parts, one of its own. Nature and its things phenomenalize through the human body, existentialize through the human body. Therefore, perception and the human body do not cut us off from the world. They are our access to it. They are the means by which the world more fully exists, by which the world is known, for the inside of the body is the internal double of the world outside upon which it opens.

If we understand the body as dehiscence, as a splitting open of the body as touching and touched, as a splitting open that puts the body in contact with the world's things but that separates them from it as well, if we understand fact and essence as presenting themselves within this opening, then we can also understand language—which displays the same kind of dehiscence between speaking and ideas.

For Merleau-Ponty, then, there is an analogy between the body and speech. The body "splits open" (dehiscence) between the body as perceiver and the body as perceived (the hand touches from the inside because it is touched from the outside). This splitting open of the body is actually what allows it to perceive the world around it, to open upon a world that folds back upon it. Speech (a form of bodily gesture) splits open as well, for it aims at a world of sublimated meanings that fold back upon it.

> As my body, which is one of the visibles, sees itself also and thereby makes itself the natural light opening its own interior to the visible, in order for the visible there to become my own landscape . . . ; so also speech (*la parole*)—which . . . is, as a constituted language (*langage*), a certain region in the universe of significations—is also the organ . . . of all other regions of signification and consequently coextensive with the thinkable. (*VI* 118)

Yet Merleau-Ponty goes on to claim even more:

> In reality, there is much more than a parallel or an analogy here, there is solidarity and intertwining: if speech, which is but a region of the intelligible world, can be also its refuge, this is because speech prolongs into the invisible, extends unto the semantic operations, the belongingness of the body to being and the corporeal relevance of every being, which for me is once and for all attested by the visible, and whose idea each intellectual evidence reflects a little further. (*VI* 118)

Active human perception, which is a kind of gesturing, and the meanings that are formed in this gesticulating encounter with the world slip into and are prolonged by the bodily gesture called speech. There is here an ontological priority granted to the body and the world upon which it opens, for together in lived experience they sustain a field of stable meanings, meanings that are then sublimated in the bodily gesture called speech.

> In a philosophy that takes into consideration the operative world, functioning, present and coherent, as it is, the essence is not at all a stumbling block: it has its place there as an operative, functioning, essence. No longer are there essences above us, like positive objects, offered to a spiritual eye; but there is an essence beneath us, a common nervure of the signifying and the signified, adherence in and reversibility of one another—as the visible things are the secret folds of our flesh, and yet our body is one of the visible things. As the world is behind my body, the operative essence is behind the operative speech also, the speech that possesses the signification less than it is possessed by it, that does not speak of *it,* but speaks *it,* or speaks *according to it,* or lets it speak and be spoken within me, breaks through my present. (*VI* 118)

Thus, just as the perceptual gestalt or meaning is formed at the intersection of the engaged body and the world's things, just as the invisible lines of force between the gestalt's background and the foreground it helps present are formed in the lived experience to which both the body and the world contribute, so also linguistic gesture or meaning is formed at the intersection of lived speech and the field of sublimated meanings. And just as there is a common gestalt or nervure between the perceiver and the perceived, there is a common nervure between the act of signification and the field of the signified. As we have seen, the nervure of perception passes into that of speech.

> As the nervure bears the leaf from within, from the depths of the flesh, the ideas are the texture of experience, its style, first mute, then uttered. Like every style, they are elaborated within the thickness of being and, not only in fact but also by right, could not be detached from it, to be spread out on display under the gaze. (*VI* 119)

In "Indirect Language and the Voices of Silence," Merleau-Ponty states that the painter's style is not within him (or her) but is a certain manner of meeting the world, a certain way of being in the world, a certain corporeal schema for confronting the world. (See *Signs* 53–54.) This style is not *created.* It is at first discovered in the painter's acts, in his or her corporeal way of organizing the world. It can be developed and elaborated, but only within being, for it is only a way of meeting being. Thus, since artistic gesture and linguistic gesture are comparable for Merleau-Ponty, both are rooted in being and are, at the same time, a prolongation of it, for both organize it in meaningful ways. Furthermore, the act of gesturing itself (either perceptual or linguistic) can never be fully perceived because the act of reflection reduces it to an object, thus losing sight of the act as lived. This, once again, expresses the embodiment of speech. Speech like consciousness is embodied, and speech like consciousness refers primarily to the world—a world that can nevertheless be sublated and expressed in more abstract and literary forms.

Merleau-Ponty not only opposes idealistic philosophy's *direct* intuition of separate ideal essences, as we have just witnessed above, he also opposes Bergson's direct intuition of the existent as immediate coincidence or fusion with the thing, to which we now turn below. First, the lack of fusion with the thing is no accident, since dehiscence is a characteristic of Being itself (as we shall see below). Second, even if fusion were established, it would bear the effort needed to accomplish it and would therefore not be immediate, total fusion, for the effort must be accomplished over time and may well be distorting. Third, if coincidence has no need for the *operations* that establish it, if it has no need for the human capacities and functions that accomplish it, then coincidence is indeed impossible for human beings who know only through them. Fourth, if fusion with the thing is total, then as a knower, as an experiencer "I cease to be," for I have collapsed into the object. I have become one with the thing. Furthermore, "in the measure that I am, there is no thing, but only a double of it in my 'camera obscura' " (*VI* 122).

After stating these criticisms, Merleau-Ponty goes on to positively state his own position:

> There is an experience of the visible thing as pre-existing my vision, but this experience is not a fusion, a coincidence: because my eyes which see, my hands which touch, can also be seen and touched, because, therefore, in this sense they see and touch the visible, the tangible, from within, because our flesh lines and even envelops all the visible and tangible things with which nevertheless it is surrounded, the world and I are within one another, and there is no anteriority of the *percipere* to the *percipi,* there is simultaneity or even retardation. For the weight of the natural world is already a weight of the past. (*VI* 123)

In this important and somewhat confusing passage, we observe Merleau-Ponty expressing the experience of a preexistent visible, thus granting an ontological priority to the visible world. We also observe Merleau-Ponty moving on to immediately state that there is no anteriority of perception to the perceived, that they are simultaneous, given at the same time. Yet he just as quickly moves on to claim that there is a retardation, a slowness or slipping away of the natural world into the past. We must first remember that this is a first rough draft, that ideas are being expressed freely and quickly. Yet Merleau-Ponty at his worst is often better than most at their best, and what we have here is certainly open to reasonable interpretation, especially with the aid of context. Within the context of Merleau-Ponty's philosophy, one must always begin with lived experience. This lived experience is embodied. It is centered in a body that opens immediately out unto a world. In this sense, the perception and perceived are given simultaneously. To experience means to be an embodied subject opening simultaneously upon a really existent world. Yet as an experiencer, experiences temporally slip away from me and thus open to a world prior to me. This can be observed in the way Merleau-Ponty continues the above passage:

> Each landscape of my life, because it is not a wandering troop of sensations or a system of ephemeral judgments but a segment of the durable flesh of the world, is qua visible, pregnant with many other visions besides my own; and the visible that I see, of which I speak . . . is numerically the same that Plato and Aristotle saw and spoke of. (*VI* 123)

Yet for Merleau-Ponty, this *transcendence* of the world is only given *within* experience. We can never get outside of the avenues of experience (the human body and its eyes, hands, and so on) to perceive a world in itself. We necessarily experience the world through the human body, yet this experience opens out to a world that runs beyond it.

> When I find again the actual world such as it is, under my hands, under my eyes, up against my body, I find much more than an object: a Being of which my vision is a part, a visibility older than my operation or my acts. But this does not mean that there was a fusion or coinciding of me with it: on the contrary, this occurs because a sort of dehiscence opens my body in two, and because between my body looked at and my body looking, my body touched and my body touching, there is overlapping or encroachment, so that we must say that the things pass into us as well as we into the things. (*VI* 123)

For Merleau-Ponty, there is a sort of internal contact with the visible world, for my body, my flesh experienced from the inside opens immediately to a world outside. My hand touches from the inside because it is touched from the outside. There is a chiasm: the inside passes or crosses into the outside as the outside passes into the inside. And yet, this chiasm cannot be complete. There cannot be total fusion, for then the experiencer and the experienced would conflate, would become one, thereby making experience impossible. There must be an experience that puts us in contact with the world outside and yet separates us from it, keeps us at a distance from it. And there is of course such an experience, an experience which is grounded in the human body, in the body as a two-dimensional being. This body is lived through, is phenomenal, is experienced from the inside as it opens to the outside. Yet this body is also experienced from the outside, is seen or touched from the outside. These two dimensions are never coincident. They slip away from each other continuously. In fact, it is the opening between the body as touching and the body as touched, as perceiving and as perceived that actually makes experience possible, that opens the body to the *awareness* of the outside world. The lack of coincidence *and* the lack of total separation (for total separation would make experience impossible as well, since the body as touching and the body as touched would pass each other like two ships in the night) between the two aspects of the body are what makes human experience possible. Experiencing (or perception) is a contact that remains at a distance. From this, Merleau-Ponty is able to conclude the following: "Like the philosophies of reflection, what Bergson lacks is the double reference, the identity of the retiring into oneself with the leaving of oneself, of the lived through with the distance" (*VI* 124). Lived-through experience occurs within the body as it simultaneously opens to a world. The lived contact with oneself is simultaneously the lived contact with the things that are separate from oneself, that are at a distance from oneself.

> If the coincidence is never but partial, we must not define the truth by total or effective coincidence. And if we have the idea of the thing itself, there must be something in the factual order that answers to it. It is therefore necessary that the deflecting (*écart*), without which the experience of the thing or of the past would fall to zero, be also an openness upon the thing itself, to the past itself, that it enter into their definition. (*VI* 124)

> What there is is not a coinciding by principle or a presumptive coinciding and a factual non-coinciding, a bad or abortive truth, but a privative non-coinciding from afar, a divergence and something like a "good error." (*VI* 124–25)

It is the human body, then, as a two-dimensional being, that carries me to the things and puts me in contact with them where they rest, and yet that also separates me from them. Our theories of truth must therefore account for this bodily contact at a distance, this "good error," and abandon the idea of total coincidence or total separation.

A consideration of language leads us to a better understanding of coincidence, for if coincidence is total fusion with the thing, then language can only cut us off from this fusion, for it would act as a means or an instrument that expresses the thing yet simultaneously separates us from it, that distorts the thing as it is purely in itself (*VI* 125). Yet philosophers speak; they attempt to express their mute contact with the world. However, they also realize that language cannot articulate this silence because by its very nature it takes it up and expresses it. Language seems to add to or leave out or distort the original mute contact with Being. Yet philosophers continue to speak; they continue to try again, to try to get closer. This renewal indicates both that speech does seem to be getting closer to Being and yet also seems to deviate from it. Perhaps then language lies somewhere between total coincidence and total deception (*VI* 125).

> We need only to take language in the living or nascent state . . . Language is a life, is our life and the life of things. Not that *language* takes possession of life and reserves it for itself: what would there be to say if there existed nothing but things said? It is the error of the semantic philosophies to close up language as if it spoke only of itself: language lives only from silence; everything we cast to the others has germinated in this great mute land which we never leave. (*VI* 125–26)

Even though Merleau-Ponty does not specifically identify the above-mentioned "semantic philosophies," his statement here definitely puts him at odds with deconstructionists such as Derrida, who claim that language is nothing but signifiers constantly deferring to other signifiers, and with those who interpret *The Visible and the Invisible* as a deconstructionist text. For Merleau-Ponty, even in this last text, language opens upon a mute visible world that it has its origins in and that it continues to refer to. Merleau-Ponty continues:

> But, because he has experienced within himself the need to speak, the birth of speech as bubbling up at the bottom of his mute experience, the philosopher knows better than anyone that what is lived is lived-spoken, that, born at this depth, language is not a mask over Being, but—if one knows how to grasp it with all its roots and all its foliation—the most valuable witness to Being, that it does not interrupt an immediation that

> would be perfect without it, that the vision itself, the thought itself, are as has been said, "structured as a language," are *articulation* before the letter, apparition of something where there was nothing or something else. (*VI* 126)

Notice that Merleau-Ponty says here, quoting Lacan's phrase, that vision and thought are "structured as a language," yet it is clear from the immediate context (and from a wider context, to be explicated below) that the visible is primary, that language is structured as it is because visual experience is structured as it is. Language is diacritical because visual experience is gestaltlike and therefore diacritical.

> Hence the problem of language is, if one likes, only a regional problem—that is, if we consider the ready-made language, the secondary and empirical operation of translation, of coding and decoding, the artificial languages, the technical relation between a sound and a meaning which are joined only by express convention and are therefore ideally isolable. (*VI* 126)

In other words, language can be and often is treated as a special topic, and as an object, for study by the empirical sciences. Yet a different view of language emerges if we consider it from the point of view of the language user.

> But if, on the contrary, we consider the speaking word, the assuming of the conventions of his native language as something natural by him who lives within that language, the folding over within him of the visible and the lived experience upon language, and of language upon the visible and the lived experience, the exchanges between the articulations of his mute language and those of his speech, finally that operative language which has no need to be translated into significations and thoughts, that language-thing which counts as an arm, as action, as offense and as seduction because it brings to the surface all the deep-rooted relations of the lived experience wherein it takes form, and which is the language of life and of action but also that of literature and of poetry—then this logos is an absolutely universal theme, it is the theme of philosophy. (*VI* 126)

The above claim leaves little doubt that language takes form in lived experience, that "it brings to the surface all the deep-rooted relations of the lived experience wherein it takes form." It is true, as deconstructionist interpretations claim, that Merleau-Ponty claims that language helps articulate experience, that language folds back on the visual field and covers it everywhere with linguistic significations. Yet this is only half the truth, for language is first born in our lived-through perceptual contact with the world; it is at first a taking up of the mute perceptual gesture and its visual field in order to express them more fully. Language is at first the voice of the things as they come to expression in our lived-through perceptual encounter with the world. We will observe this more closely below, yet moving on to discuss the relationship between language and philosophy, Merleau-Ponty expresses the point clearly here as well.

> Philosophy itself is language, rests on language; but this does not disqualify it from speaking of language, nor from speaking of the pre-language and of the mute world which doubles them: on the contrary, philosophy is an operative language, that language that can be known only from within, through its exercise, is open upon the things, called forth by the voices of silence, and continues an effort of articulation which is the Being of every being. (*VI* 126–27)

Philosophy, then, is neither intuition of essences nor fusion/coincidence with the things. Both of these types of philosophy are errors. Both are forms of positivism, both expect the object to be fully present, as an ideal or as an existent thing. Both forget "that every being presents itself at a distance, which does not prevent us from knowing, which is on the contrary the guarantee for knowing it" (*VI* 127). Both forget

> that our openness, our fundamental relationship with Being, that which makes it impossible for us to feign to not be, could not be formed in the order of the being-posited, since it is this openness precisely that teaches us that the beings-posited, whether true or false, are not nothing, that, whatever be the experience, an experience is always contiguous upon an experience, that our perceptions, our judgments, our sole knowledge of the world can be changed, crossed out, Husserl says, but not nullified, that, under the doubt that strikes them appear other perceptions, other judgments more true, because we are within Being and because there is something. (*VI* 128)

Merleau-Ponty concludes his discourse on the philosophies of reflection and coincidence by claiming that what we need is not a philosophy of essence or coincidence, not another form of positivism, but not its opposite either, not a total negation or nothingness. What is called for is a "theory of the philosophical view or vision as a maximum of the true proximity to a Being in dehiscence" (*VI* 128). Merleau-Ponty will answer this call in the last chapter of *The Visible and the Invisible* that he was able to complete, to which I now turn.

2

The Visible

"The Intertwining—the Chiasm"

Since both the philosophy of reflection and the philosophy of coincidence fail to adequately describe experience, Merleau-Ponty says, in the last partially completed chapter of *The Visible and the Invisible,* we must return to it and describe it anew, describe it prior to the bifurcation of subject and object, essence and existence. In this chapter, more than in any other of Merleau-Ponty's writings, the author attempts to develop a new descriptive terminology, a terminology that does not represent the old dichotomies of Western philosophy and Western culture, that will more fully integrate subject and object, but without the complete immersion of one into the other. Merleau-Ponty here repeats what he has expressed earlier about the paradox of perception, now in the form of a question: "What is . . . this singular virtue of the visible that makes it, held at the end of the gaze, nonetheless much more than a correlative of my vision, such that it imposes my vision upon me as a continuation of its own sovereign existence?" (*VI* 131). How is it that we both see the things where they rest yet see them also as correlations to our vision? After several critical chapters, summarized above, where this question was explored with respect to other philosophies and where we witnessed some provisional statements of his view, Merleau-Ponty now gives full expression to his own answer: "It is that the look is itself incorporation of the seer into the visible—it is as flesh offered to flesh that the visible has its aseity, and that it is mine" (*VI* 131, note).

Against Descartes, Merleau-Ponty has said in an earlier work (*PhP* 374 f.) that the existential modality of the perceiver and the perceived is the same, that one cannot doubt the object perceived while accepting the certainty of the act of perception that supposedly reveals this object. To be sure of the act of perception is to be sure of reaching the object perceived, for what it means to perceive is to reach an existent object, to have the object's existence revealed to the perceiver in this act. In "The Philosopher and Sociology" ("PS," 166 f.), completed about the time he started *The Visible and the Invisible,* Merleau-Ponty says that there is a special relationship of the body to itself that makes it a linking bond with things. Since the body can touch itself touching, since the touching hand is present at the advent of touching in the touched hand, the body is aware of itself as a touching or perceiving thing. The body is the thing that experiences its existence from the inside. The body is able to experience the existence of things as they reveal themselves to the body because it is one of them, because it has the same thickness and bodilyness that they do. There must be a kinship between the touch and the touched in order for the touch to open upon the tangible world. The hand which touches from the inside must be capable of being touched from the outside. It must take its place in the tangible world. "Through this crisscrossing within [the hand] of the touching and the tangible, its own movements incorporate themselves into the universe they interrogate" (*VI* 133). The hand incorporates itself into the world just as the world is incorporated into the movement of the hand. "If the body is one sole body, in its two phases, it incorporates into itself the whole of its sensible and with the same movement incorporates itself into a 'Sensible in itself' " (*VI* 138). "We can understand then why we see the things themselves, in their place, where they are, according to their being which is indeed more than a being-perceived" (*VI* 135). It is because they are bodies which we as *incarnate beings* are *among.* The human body is like them. It is one of them. It has a place among them where they rest. And yet we also understand "why at the same time we are separated from them by all the thickness of the look and the body; it is that this distance is not the contrary of this proximity, it is deeply consonant with it, it is synonymous with it. It is that the thickness of the flesh between the seer and the thing is constitutive for the thing of its visibility as for the seer of his corporeity" (*VI* 135). We are separate from them because of the thickness of the body, because there is no pure mind or consciousness that would form a complete union or coincidence with the thing. The body is separate from the things because even though it is one of them, it is also different from them. It is the thing that is *aware* of its own existence and the existence of things. It is a *sensing* thing. (But again, it experiences their *existence* and its own because it is a thing, because it is a body.) This splitting open of the body as sensing and sensed is what allows it to open upon things, is what makes it the natural light which reveals things where they rest, as well as what separates it from the things, places it at a distance from them, for the perception occurs within the body. "It is the body and it alone, because it is a two-dimensional being, that can bring us to the things themselves" and that keeps us at a distance from them (*VI* 136).

We must of course remember that this separateness is not the separateness of a reflective or transcendent consciousness. It is the body's reflexivity that allows it to open itself to (and keeps it at a distance from) the world around it, the world that it is embedded in.

> There is vision, touch, when a certain visible, a certain tangible, turns back upon the whole of the visible/tangible of which it is a part, or when between it and them, and through their commerce, is formed a visibility, a tangible in itself. (*VI* 139)

> It is this Visibility, this generality of the Sensible in itself, this anonymity innate to Myself that we have previously called flesh. (*VI* 139)

This flesh is neither matter nor idea. It is not matter in itself because it is an *aware* turning over of an active bit of matter on itself and onto the world, a turning over that organizes a visible and tangible field. It is not an idea or a representation because they would not allow themselves to descend into being, to blend with it and be incorporated into it, to be captured by it (*VI* 139). The flesh is a sort of element (like the classical terms "used to speak of water, air, earth, and fire"), "a general thing, midway between the spatio-temporal individual and the idea, a sort of incarnate principle that brings a style of being whenever there is a fragment of being" (*VI* 139). This is a "new type of being," a lived-through blending of the incarnate subject and the world, a world that nevertheless runs beyond the subject. This element, this Visibility in general, this anonymous visibility "prevails over every momentary discordance." "In advance every vision . . . that would here definitely come to naught is not nullified (which would leave a gap in its place), but what is better, it is replaced by a more exact vision and a more exact visible" (*VI* 140). One visible can be substituted for another, not just as its negation but as its *replacement*. Therefore some visible always remains, as does a visibility in general, as does Being. With this Merleau-Ponty has stated his understanding of the meaning of being. It is that which presents itself as existent in its own right, yet which also appears at the end of our gaze. This no longer expresses the paradox observed above because we now see that it is the special structure of the human body, its belongingness to the world and the world's things and its reflexive distance from them, that delivers both experiences at the same time.

Yet this does not answer all ontological questions. We need now to turn to the existence of other persons and to the existence of language and ideas.

> It is said that the colors, the tactile reliefs given to the other, are for me an absolute mystery, forever inaccessible. This is not completely true; for me to have not an idea, image nor a representation, but as it were the imminent experience of them, it suffices that I look at a landscape, that I speak of it with someone. Then, through the concordant operation of his body and my own, what I see passes into him, this individual green of the meadow under my eyes invades his vision without quitting my own, I recognize in my green, his green . . . There is no problem of the *alter ego* because it is not *I* who sees, not *he* who sees, because an anonymous visibility inhabits both of us, a vision in general, in virtue of that primordial property that belongs to the flesh, being here and now, of radiating everywhere and forever, being an individual, of being also a dimension and a universal. (*VI* 142)

Since, for Merleau-Ponty, consciousness is not the Cartesian private awareness of the contents of one's own mind but a bodily relationship to the world, a dehiscence of the body that throws the body (*ek-stace*) out of itself toward the world, then experiencing someone else's experience becomes much less problematic—since embodied consciousnesses gesturing toward the world must meet at the thing, overlap at the object. We must remember that this occurs at the prereflective level. It is indeed impossible to experience someone else's *thought,* those private ideas behind the other's reflective gaze. Yet "I know unquestionably that that man over there *sees,* that my sensible world is also his, because *I am present at his seeing,* it *is visible* in his eyes' grasp of the scene" ("PS" 169). "What I perceive" then "is a different 'sensibility' (*Empfindbarkeit*), and only subsequently a different man and different thought." And this perception of the other is prepared by my own body, for when the body touches itself, when one hand touches the other, the touching hand experiences the touched hand as an object, yet it also experiences the advent of touching in the touched hand. Merleau-Ponty believes that this experience of the advent of awareness in the touched hand can be extended to others. There is a sort of extension of my own copresence to the other ("PS" 168). There is thus an intersubjective, or, rather, an intercorporeal being. At this level of prereflective perception there is an awareness of other embodied subjects who perceptually open upon a common world. "What is open to us, therefore, with the reversibility of the visible and the tangible, is—if not yet the incorporeal—at least an intercorporeal being, a presumptive domain of the visible and the tangible, which extends further than the things I touch and see at present" (*VI* 142–43).

Moving now to the "incorporeal," to the "invisible" realm of the ideal meanings of language, Merleau-Ponty makes the following claim:

> The reversibility that defines the flesh exists in other fields . . . As there is a reflexivity of the touch, of sight, and of the touch-vision system, there is a reflexivity of the movements of phonation and of hearing. (*VI* 144)

> This new reversibility and the emergence of the flesh as expression are the point of insertion of speaking and thinking in the world of silence. (*VI* 144–45)

As we observed above, for Merleau-Ponty perception is already meaningful and is already a gesture. Because perception is active, interested, engaged, it confronts the world in a lived-through interaction that produces a meaning. This meaning is a gestalt, an organized field, with a foreground and a background, an identity within the context of difference, a presence in the context of an absence. There is thus a perceptual ideality, an armature of the perceptual gestalt (to which both the embodied perceiver and the world contribute) that remains "hidden." The "lines" or "forces" of the perceptual gestalt field help articulate the foreground against the background but themselves remain inarticulate or without full visibility. Vocal gesture is a prolongation of this perceptual sense, of this engaged, needful encounter. As such there is a prolongation of the perceptual ideality into the pure ideality of speech. The armature or horizon of perception emigrates to a less heavy body, to the body of language, to speech.

Merleau-Ponty offers an interesting explication of this perceptual or sensual ideality—some of which he borrows from Proust. When listening to music, as a lived-through rhythm of sound, the music offers a sense, a meaningful pattern. After the event, after the fact, one can reflect and produce an abstract notation of this rhythm. One can "objectively" write down the notes. These notes or objective marks then are able to refer to the *little musical phrase,* to the sense as it was previously lived. Merleau-Ponty understands operative speech in this same way, that is, lived-through speech expresses a sense, a sense that is, as we have just observed, sublimated from the perceptual ideal. After the speech has been made, one can reflect, as linguists and grammarians do, and take notice of its structure and pattern. One can develop a taxonomy of signs and how they fit together. These signs, these marks on a page, can then refer to the lived sense as it was originally expressed.

Thus in an attempt to answer the question of how a word gets its meaning, Merleau-Ponty revealed a series of chiasms, or intersections, as is represented by the crosspiece X, the Greek letter for *chi.* First, we must remember that in this last work Merleau-Ponty characterizes the human body as dehiscence, as a splitting open, as a reflexivity, a touching that is touched, a perceiving that is perceived. These two dimensions or aspects of the body never coincide; they pivot about the body. Moreover, it is precisely the body's ability to be able to touch itself touching, to fold back upon itself, to be aware of itself that allows it to fold back upon the world, to be aware of the world. This dehiscence or splitting open therefore also holds together. It is a chiasm, a crisscrossing of the touch and the touching, of the perceiving and the perceived. As the hand touches from the inside, it is touched from the outside. The hand opens out to something that is beyond it, yet with which it partially blends. The blending can never be total because the perceiver and the perceived would conflate, would collapse into one another and become one, making experience impossible. There must be a slippage, a displacement, a distance that separates the perceiver and the perceived. The dehiscence of the body thus produces a chiasm, a crisscrossing that is never complete, a holding together that keeps a distance.

Now, to explain how a word gets its meaning, Merleau-Ponty will disclose three types of chiasm: that between the body and the world (that is, between the perceiver and the perceived); that between the perceiver and language; and that between a word and its meaning. Let us briefly consider these chiasms. For Merleau-Ponty, the body is active/passive. It actively opens upon and explores the world as it receives information from it. Human meaning is formed where the active body and the world come together or cross (chiasm). For Merleau-Ponty perception is then already meaningful; it already actively relates the parts of the perceptual field to each other to create a gestalt whole. Perception is already a meaningful gesture. Merleau-Ponty hypothesizes that words, which are another form of bodily gesture, at first express our active, interested, emotional encounter with the world. I live the world and gesture in it and toward it, and others see what I live and couple with my gestures. In addition, the human body has the power to appropriate the gestures witnessed in others and to use these gestures to express. Therefore, just as the body opens upon a perceptual world that folds back upon it, creating a meaningful gestalt, so bodily gestures, including the voice, the word, open upon a field of sublimated meanings (sublimated from the body's lived perceptual encounter with the world) that fold back upon them. There is a chiasm between the perceiver and the perceived where meaning is first formed. Then there is a chiasm between perceptual gesturing and vocal gesturing; words and other bodily gestures (such as a caress or the shaking of one's fist) express or prolong the lived-through, emotional encounter with the world and others. And finally, there is a chiasm between words and the field of meanings they express.

Consequently, just as the perceiver and the perceived fold back upon one another, just as the body and the world incorporate each other into themselves, just as the perceiver is always a part of the perceived and must be considered along with it, just as the body perceives through certain levels, certain schemas or avenues, from a certain time and place, and with certain interests, so a word and its meaning fold back upon one another, so the means of expression and the expressed form a chiasm, a system, so the means of expression and the signification it expresses have a common nervure. If we remember that Merleau-Ponty is an *existential* phenomenologist, that within the framework of his philosophy one's own existence and the existence of the perceived things are given in the body's lived encounter with the world, then we can grasp how he comes to conceive of language as he does. Meaning is first formed in this lived encounter with the world. The meaning formed in this lived-through perceptual gesturing slips into the gesturing of the body called speech. This lived-through vocal gesturing sublimates those perceptual meanings, expresses those sublimated meanings, is the natural light of language. Speech becomes a less heavy body that opens and refers to the field of meanings that fold back on the means of expression that they rely upon for their existence, yet which they nevertheless help articulate.

One's lived bodily, perceptual encounter with the world (which is a kind of expression) gives rise to speech, which in turn folds back on its means. The completed part of *The Visible and the Invisible* ends with the claim that "what we have to understand is that there is no dialectical reversal from one of these views to the other; we do not have to reassemble them into a synthesis; they are two aspects of the reversibility which is the ultimate truth" (*VI* 155). In other words, things express their existence actively through the human body, which meets the world and expresses the world's lived sense in the lived gesture called speech. These meanings fold back upon their means of expression, just as speech folds back upon perception and perception upon the world. And all of these chiasms are copresent. Yet this doesn't mean that one is not more primary. We have seen throughout that it is the lived body's active encounter with a world that is really there that is ontologically primary. (Again, see *VI* 118–19, and also 96–97. See also *PhP* 383–88.) Neither language nor "pure significations" have an ontological priority over the "there is" of the world as it is presented to the body. Both, rather, are a sublimation of it.

I should end this presentation of Merleau-Ponty's last vision with a brief look at how he now perceives the role of philosophy. Below the level of reflection and intellectual intentionality, below the level at which traditional philosophy operates, there is a level of operative, bodily intentionality that cannot be fully captured or reconstructed by thought. Beneath the pure disengaged knower and the pure thing of traditional philosophy lies the level of lived-through experience—where their separation remains problematic. It is in the lived body's encounter with the world, where there is a partial blending of the perceiver and the perceived, that meaning is formed. Within this new kind of ontology, philosophy takes on a new kind of role.

> [Philosophy] remains a question, it interrogates the world and the thing, it revives, repeats, or initiates their crystallization before us. For this crystallization which is partly given to us ready-made is in other respects never terminated, and thereby we can see how the world comes about. It takes form under the domination of certain structural laws: events let rather general powers show through, powers such as a gaze or the word, which operate according to an identifiable style. (*VI* 100)

This expresses Merleau-Ponty's notion of philosophy as an embodied existential phenomenology. As a phenomenologist he is concerned with reflectively describing lived experience. As an existential phenomenologist he is concerned with the existence of both the perceiver and the perceived as they present themselves within lived experience. And as an embodied existential phenomenologist he takes as his point of departure an embodied consciousness that is embedded in the world. And since the body is actively embedded in the world that folds back upon it, it is only here that meaning is formed. It is the task of philosophy to reflect on this emergence of meaning. In addition, since the body is concretely engaged in the world from the point of view of a particular time and place, a time and place that are continually unfolding and changing, the patterned perceptions, the different styles of different things are continually unfolding and changing. Embodied perception gives us meaningful patterns, gestalts. But as perception changes, the patterns and gestalts change and shift. Our world is a meaningful one. There are stable patterns of perception that are held together by the body and the world. Yet because both are continually changing and changing with respect to one another, the stable meanings also unfold and shift. Consequently,

> [w]e do not have a consciousness constitutive of the things, as idealism believes, nor a preordination of the things to the consciousness, as realism believes . . . —we have with our body, our senses, our look, our power to understand speech and to speak, *measurants* (*mesurants*) of Being, dimensions to which we can refer it, but not a relation of adequation or of

> immanence. The perception of the world and of history is the practice of this measure, the reading off of their divergence or of their difference with respect to our norms. If we are ourselves in question in the very unfolding of our life, . . . it is because we ourselves are one sole continued question, a perpetual enterprise of taking our bearings on the constellations of the world, and of taking the bearings of the things on our dimensions. (*VI* 103)

Within Merleau-Ponty's philosophy, the properties of a thing stand in a relationship of "I can" to the embodied motor subject, or, that is to say, the meaning of the thing is found in the body's active, interested encounter with it, is formed in the body's avenues, or dimensions, or exploratory schemas that measure the world according to favored norms of perception and behavior. Philosophy is the attempt to make sense out of our continually "taking our bearings on the constellations of the world, and of taking the bearings of things on our dimensions." Philosophy is a sort of perpetual investigation of the continual emergence of meaning in the body's perceptual encounter with the world. Philosophy is the interrogation of perceptual faith (*VI* 103). "Philosophy is the perceptual faith questioning itself about itself" (*VI* 103). It is our attempt to make sense of our continually taking our bearings in a world that is already there (*VI* 121).

> "What do I know?" is not only "what is knowing?" and not only "who am I?" but finally: "what is there?" and even: "what is the *there is?*" These questions call not for the exhibiting of something said which would put an end to them, but for the disclosure of a Being that is not posited because it has no need to be, because it is silently behind all our affirmations, negations, and even behind all formulated questions, not that it is a matter of forgetting them in our chatter, but because philosophy is the reconversion of silence and speech into one another: "It is the experience . . . still mute which we are concerned with leading to the pure expression of its own meanings." (*VI* 129: Merleau-Ponty is here quoting Husserl's *Meditations Cartesiennes* [1947], 33. English translation, *Cartesian Meditations* [1960], 38–39.)[1]

3

Nature

The Concept of Nature I

Merleau-Ponty thinks the philosophy of nature has largely been neglected and that this in turn has led to a neglect of a more fundamental philosophy of man or "spirit"—usually conceived superficially as the negation of nature. Merleau-Ponty will seek to develop a philosophy of nature that does not set nature and man ("spirit") against each other, that is not strictly materialist but that is not immaterialist either, that weaves nature and the human together (*TFL* 62).

Merleau-Ponty shows some disappointment with Marxist philosophers for whom the philosophy of nature should be of special concern. He finds that even in Marx the philosophy of nature is inadequately expressed in two forms: nature is conceived alternatively as a sum of material objects in external relationships *or* as that which is transformed by human labor and human history. The third alternative that would dialectically weave these two together, although mentioned as "objective activity," has never been adequately developed by Marx or Marxist philosophers (*TFL* 63).

It is precisely this third alternative that Merleau-Ponty seeks to develop. For nature cannot be adequately conceived as a pure thing in itself over against a pure consciousness for itself (*TFL* 64). A better way to conceive nature would be that "it is an object from which we have arisen, in which our beginnings have been posited little by little until the very moment of tying themselves to an existence which they continue to sustain and aliment" (*TFL* 64). Human existence and human consciousness thus emerge from nature and continue to be nurtured from within by nature. Human consciousness is therefore never to be conceived as a pure for itself projecting its meaning over a pure in itself. For even though human perceptions are subsequently filled with human meanings, Merleau-Ponty claims that "however surcharged with historical significations man's perception may be, it borrows from the primordial at least its manner of presenting the object and its ambiguous evidence. Nature . . . 'is there from the first day.' It presents itself always as already there before us, and yet as new before the gaze" (*TFL* 65). Thus even though Merleau-Ponty clearly recognizes the human tendencies to project historical, cultural, and linguistic meanings into perception, nature is always already there as primordially given within perception and as continually nurturing the abstract significations of our cultural and linguistic world.

Furthermore, against the idealists, Merleau-Ponty goes on to assert that "reflexive thought is disoriented by this implication of the immemorial in the present." For in idealist thought "each moment of the world ceases to be present and is only held in past being by reflective thought" (*TFL* 65). "If we are not resigned to saying that a world from which consciousness is cut off is nothing at all, then in some way we must recognize that primordial being which is not yet the subject-being nor the object-being and which in every respect baffles reflection" (*TFL* 65).

Clearly these initial comments already place Merleau-Ponty's philosophy of nature squarely between the materialist view of a nature in itself and the idealist view that tends to make the meaning of nature only the product of reflective consciousness.

Continuing his analysis, Merleau-Ponty notes that "we can neither conceive of primordial being engendering itself, which would make it infinite, nor think of it being engendered by another, which would reduce it to the condition of a product and dead result. Such is our problem" (*TFL* 66). Before Merleau-Ponty himself tries to solve this problem he will retrace the steps it has taken in the recent history of philosophy. More specifically, he will retrace the steps he thinks Husserl has taken through modern and contemporary philosophy (*TFL* 79). The exposition that follows will use Merleau-Ponty's section headings from the relevant portions of the *Themes from the Lectures.*

Elements of Our Concept of Nature

In a brief untitled introductory section, Merleau-Ponty simply states that he will begin with Descartes because a " 'Cartesian' conception . . . still overhangs contemporary ideas about nature" (*TFL* 67).

The Cartesian Idea of Nature

Descartes's ontology gives full expression to the alternatives of being and nothingness, for on the one hand, nature is conceived as a thing in itself, as necessary laws of external cause and effect—to which even God must submit. Yet on the other hand, nature is also conceived as coming out of nothing, as created by God, who is *causa sui*. In fact, "the world might not have existed had God not decided to create it; it therefore arose from a 'before' in which nothing or no preponderant possibility prefigured it or called it into existence. But once the world had arisen, it is necessitated to be such as we see it" (*TFL* 67).

Merleau-Ponty believes this ontology has its limits: since for Descartes nature is revealed to humanity through the understanding, yet because of "the contingency of the act of creation, Descartes upheld the facticity of nature and thus legitimized another perspective," that which humans have through the contingency of their own lived-through bodies. "It is life which validly comprehends the life of the human composite. But how can we leave the definition of being and truth to pure understanding if it is not grounded so as to know the existent world?" (*TFL* 70). Descartes's ontology thus fails to reconcile the pure understanding with the comprehension that is grounded in the contingency of life.

Kantian Humanism and Nature

Merleau-Ponty next briefly considers Kant and remarks that Kant is similar to Descartes in that his philosophy of nature is "coordinated by categories of the understanding" (*TFL* 71). Yet what Merleau-Ponty finds interesting in Kant is his attempt to go beyond this kind of "anthropological thinking" in his analysis of the organism. Merleau-Ponty comments on this analysis:

> The organism, in which every event is cause and effect of all others, and in this sense cause of itself, raises the problem of an auto-production of the whole, or, more precisely, of a totality which, in contrast with human technique, works upon materials which are its very own and, so to speak, emanates from them. It seems that within an entity that is in the world one encounters a mode of liaison which is not the connection of external causality, that is, an "interior" unlike the interior of consciousness, and thus nature must be something other than an object. (*TFL* 71)

Thus, even though Kant seems to recognize natural wholes not coordinated by the understanding and the internal relations of conceptual meaning, he is left with the problem of how "these natural totalities" are grounded (*TFL* 72), and, says Merleau-Ponty, Kant ultimately "considers the 'natural end' as" expressing the *human need* to organize the contingently given, thus returning to anthropological thinking (*TFL* 72–73).

Essays on the Philosophy of Nature

Merleau-Ponty next considers Schelling, who is critical of Descartes's idea of a necessary being, and, in fact, refers to it as the "abyss of human reason." For Schelling there is no rational ground or origin of nature. Rather the abyss (or the absolute) is itself without reason and is the groundless ground for "the grand fact of the world" (*TFL* 72). In addition, Schelling rejects Kant's idea that the natural totalities can be explained by reference to human judgment. Merleau-Ponty observes that what we see developing in Schelling is an "intellectual intuition"—"which is not an occult faculty, but perception as it is before it has been reduced to ideas; it is perception dormant within itself, in which all things are me because I am not yet the reflecting subject" (*TFL* 75). Yet this ordinary knowledge is brought into existence by man and by the distance that human reflection is able to take on nature (*TFL* 75–76). Even though Schelling's view of perception bears a certain resemblance to Merleau-Ponty's, the latter offers the following objection:

> It is clear, however, that [Schelling's] "doctrine of reflection," or the mirror, leaves nature in the state of an *object* which we reflect, and that, if philosophy is to avoid immaterialism, it must establish a more strict relation between man and nature than this looking-glass relation, since nature and consciousness can only truly communicate in us and through our incarnate being. (*TFL* 76–77)

For Merleau-Ponty consciousness cannot be a detached spiritual or intellectual mirror or reflection. It is intertwined with the body, which is intertwined with the world. Any understanding of the relationship between consciousness and the world must therefore account for this intertwining, this "familiarity." Schelling's understanding does not.

Next commenting on Bergson, Merleau-Ponty finds the following points of interest. Bergson does not seek to reproduce in *reflection* (as Schelling does) that which is *perceptually given*. Rather, pure perception seems to reach the thing as it is in itself. Yet Bergson also seems to recognize (at least unconsciously) that there is no pure perception, for, within philosophy, the only way to have an articulated perception is against the background of the inarticulate or the indeterminate. The only way to have an articulated present is against the background of some distant field. In fact, in Merleau-Ponty's reading of Bergson, Bergson conceives of nature "as a horizon from which we are already far away, a primordial lost undividedness" (*TFL* 78). Furthermore, Bergson considers the idea of natural production, of a production that proceeds from the whole to its parts but that is not the production of an idea, when he introduces his notion of an élan vital. Yet he contradicts his own analysis of these *concrete totalities* when he conceives of the élan as possessing a reality of its own. And finally, according to Merleau-Ponty, Bergson's focus on the perceptual intuition of nature is an affirmation of the "pre-existence of natural beings, always already there" (*TFL* 79).

Merleau-Ponty's preceding historical analysis has traced the conceptual path taken by Husserl, who having started with reflection (much like Descartes) returned to a philosophy of nature, to a nature already there prior to reflection. A brief look at Merleau-Ponty's interpretation of Husserl reveals a Husserlian philosophy that looks very much like Merleau-Ponty's.

First of all, Husserl recognizes that "objective being envelops everything," even the consciousness of the philosopher, for this consciousness is part of the objective world. Yet he also recognizes that incorporating consciousness into nature, in treating it as a "pure thing," is to adopt a purely reflective, theoretical attitude—which is a form of idealism. In an avoidance of this idealism, Husserl claims that one must return to and consider the prereflective relationship between consciousness and thing, to the intuitive perceptual relationship upon which the theoretical level rests, and that an attempt must be made to understand how we move from the prereflective to the reflective. In addition, to understand the intuitive perceptual relationship, one must understand perception as embodied. Perceptual consciousness is incarnate, and must be grasped as a motor power, as an active projection into the world, as an "I can."

The focus on embodied consciousness and active perception is certainly present in Merleau-Ponty's philosophy as well, and continuing his exposition of Husserl, Merleau-Ponty points to another theme that is central to his own philosophy.

> My body is a "field of localization" in which sensations are set up. In the act of exploring objects my right hand touches my left hand, touches it touching, and in this encounters "a feeling thing." Since there is a body-subject and since it is before this that objects exist, they are virtually incorporated in my flesh. (*TFL* 80–81)

Merleau-Ponty finds here in Husserl hints of what Merleau-Ponty will develop into a full-blown ontology of the flesh.

As he continues his analysis of Husserl, Merleau-Ponty agrees with Husserl that embodied subjects also have a tendency to project around them a world of pure things, "forgetting the density of the corporeal 'pre-constitution' which sustains them" (*TFL* 81). Yet my body considered alone is not enough to account for the appearance of the pure object, for the object is still enmeshed in my corporeality and there is not yet a clear distinction between its needs and the object's properties. Moreover, my body itself has not yet been conceived as an object, and this can occur only with the appearance of another bodily consciousness—who is able to perceive me, and with whom the world can now appear as purely objective. This objective world appears because

> [t]he experience which I have of my own body as a field of localization of an experience and that which I have of other bodies in so far as they *behave* in front of me, come before one another and pass into one another. There are two properties which illumine one another and are fulfilled together. On the one hand, there is the perception which I have of my body as the seat of a "vision," of a "touch," and (since the senses flow together in it to their source in the impalpable consciousness from which they arise) of the perception of an *I think*. On the other hand, there is the perception which I have deep down of another "excitable," "sensible" body which (since all that does not occur without an *I think*) is the bearer of another *I think*. (*TFL* 81–82)

The appearance of other subjects allows for the appearance of the pure thing, of a thing that is not just the perception of a single subject. Yet according to the way Merleau-Ponty interprets Husserl here, the pure thing appears "only as the correlative of an ideal community of embodied subjects, of an intercorporeality" (*TFL* 82). There is thus a perspective beneath the pure thing as it appears to reflective thought that allows it to appear as such.

> [Husserl] sketches the description of those pre-objective beings which are the correlates of a community of perceiving bodies and stakes out its primordial history. Beneath Cartesian nature, which theoretical activity sooner or later constructs, there emerges an anterior stratum . . . Husserl risks the description of the earth as the seat of pre-objective spatiality and temporality, as the homeland and historicity of bodily subjects who are not disengaged observers, as the ground of truth or the ark which carries into the future the seeds of knowledge and culture. Before being manifest and "objective," truth dwells in the secret order of embodied subjects. At the root and in the depths of Cartesian nature there is another nature, the domain of "originary presence" (*Urpräsenz*) which, from the fact that it calls for the total response of a single embodied subject, is in principle present also to every other embodied subject. (*TFL* 82–83)

Merleau-Ponty's characterization here of Husserl's philosophy is remarkably similar to the philosophy toward which Merleau-Ponty was moving near the end of his life, that we have seen expressed in the partially completed chapters of *The Visible and the Invisible,* and that we will see further developed below. Merleau-Ponty ends his historical analysis with the claim that Husserl "recovers through the very exercise of reflexive vigor a natural stratum in the concordant functioning of bodies within brute being." Husserl's philosophy, itself very aware of the history of recent European philosophy, once "again confronts nature as an oriented and blind productivity." Yet for Merleau-Ponty this oriented and blind productivity is not to be understood, as it usually is, as a return to a teleological view of nature. "Natural production has to be understood in some other way" (*TFL* 83). It is to this new understanding that Merleau-Ponty now turns his attention.

Contemporary Science and the Signs of a New Conception of Nature

In this brief section, Merleau-Ponty argues that there is no need to extensively justify the turn toward science in the analysis of a philosophy of nature, for even though science confronts nature in a highly specialized way, by means of the algorithm, it does at least confront it. It reveals at least a narrow band of it. Yet Merleau-Ponty expresses a reservation about the philosopher's turn toward science, for philosophers lack professional competency in science and therefore should not try to intervene to resolve scientific issues. On the other hand, and this favors the philosopher's intervention, disputes between scientists often involve philosophical disputes and or philosophical interpretations. From these insights Merleau-Ponty concludes the following:

> Philosophers must find a way nicely between conceit and capitulation. This would involve asking science not what being is (science calculates *within being*, its constant procedure is to suppose the unknown known) but what being is certainly not; it would mean a scientific critique of the common notions outside of which philosophy cannot, on any hypothesis, establish itself. Science would contribute, as some physicists have said, "negative philosophical findings." (*TFL* 85)

It seems then that science itself has increasingly moved away from the Laplacean view of the universe—where all physical events are calculated and positively determined within Cartesian coordinates—for science helps determine what is not the case, not what is necessarily the case. Wave mechanics, to cite a specific example, has increasingly moved away from the view of a completely determined universe. Merleau-Ponty believes, however, that this in no way provides evidence for the opposing claim of an acausal universe, and he once again appeals to the experience of perception to offer a positive expression of a world that falls between the totally determined and the totally indeterminate. "For the perceived world is a world where there is a discontinuity, where there is probability and generality, where each being is not constrained to a unique and fixed location, to an absolute density of being" (*TFL* 86). The perceived world is thus replete with stable patterns, yet there are gaps between these patterns, which, moreover, compete with one another for attention and break up over time. Merleau-Ponty's perceptual world, the world toward which he sees contemporary science moving, is thus not the Cartesian or Laplacean world of modernism (nor is it the arbitrarily constructed world of postmodernism).

Merleau-Ponty proceeds to make similar comments about the scientific move away from the classical treatment of both space and time.

> Similarly, the scientific critique of the forms of space and time in non-Euclidean geometry and relativity physics have taught us to break with the common notion of space and time without reference to the observer's situation and enable us to give full ontological significance to certain descriptions of perceived space and time—to polymorphous space and time of which common sense and science retain only a few traces. (*TFL* 86)

For human beings there is no purely objective space, for this would presuppose a view from nowhere (or everywhere), which of course is impossible for human beings to actually achieve and perhaps impossible to even conceive. Space is always experienced by an embodied, situated observer. As it is so perceived, space is experienced as a non-Euclidean voluminosity that gradually bends around the perceiver. The Cartesian coordinate system that has become identified with the modern view and representation of space is an abstract construction of a more primitive voluminosity that is offered all at once to the embodied perceiver. Merleau-Ponty is not claiming that this abstract coordinate system is false or that we should rid ourselves of it, only that it is abstract and rests upon a more primary and open view of space.

He proceeds to make similar claims about time as well:

> Nor need the critique of absolute simultaneity in relativity physics necessarily lead to the paradoxes of the radical plurality of times—it might prepare the way for the recognition of a preobjective temporality which is universal in its own way. Perceived time is, of course, solidary with the observer's point of view, but by this fact it constitutes the common

> dimension for all possible observers of one and the same nature. And this is so, not because we are constituted so as only to attribute to other observers an expanded or foreshortened time relative to our own—but rather the very contrary, in the sense that in its singularity our perceived time announces to us other singularities and other perceived times, with the same rights as ours, and in principle grounds the philosophical similarity of a community of observers. (*TFL* 86–87)

For Merleau-Ponty, the personal awareness of time (which is needed, otherwise there would be no awareness of the *passing* of time) fuses or blends with a transcendent time (which is required for time to be deployed and not just set out spatially before a constituting subject). It does so because it is based on an incarnate perception, a perception which itself is *ek-stace,* a leaping out of itself. For Merleau-Ponty consciousness is not closed in on itself, as it has been in the Cartesian tradition, but is a bodily perception, the body's openness out onto the world. Since at the prereflective level human perceptual functions are anonymous, since these bodily functions carry me anonymously into the world, perception is a leaping out of itself toward a transcendent world that includes it and others. Bodily perception opens out unto a world that runs beyond it, yet with which it always remains in contact. In the same way the present moment of time opens upon (*ek-stace*) a transcendent past and future with which it remains in contact. It is this experience of embodied perception and of time that enables the perceiver to open to a shared world that is always already there and that is always already there for everyone. Thus, Merleau-Ponty can conclude: "In place of Laplace's dogmatic objectivity, we glimpse an objectivity pledged upon the inherence of all thinking subjects in the same core of being which remains amorphous but with whose presence they experiment from within the situation to which they belong" (*TFL* 87). Embodied perceptual consciousnesses open upon one sole world, yet they always do so through concrete experimental situations. As individuals and groups adapt to the world through these concrete situations, they uncover a world that has always already been there. Yet it has always been there for engaged *embodied subjects* as a realm of common activity, not for a pure intellectual consciousness as a pure thing in itself. It is this lived-through perceptual world that should therefore be the foundation of science, and it is toward this lived-through perceptual world that science itself seems to be moving.

Moreover, the situations, scientific or otherwise, through which engaged consciousnesses encounter the world, continue to change and unfold, leading to the idea of a process or history of nature—which Merleau-Ponty addresses in the next set of courses on the life sciences.

The Concept of Nature II: Animality, the Human Body, Transition to Culture

Summarizing his next course notes, Merleau-Ponty states that "the study of nature is here an introduction to the definition of being"—which, he claims, must proceed indirectly. That is to say, ontology proceeds "up to being in general only through particular beings," and it raises questions about being only within "certain sectors of being" (*TFL* 88).

Proceeding with his analysis, Merleau-Ponty once again offers Descartes as a pertinent example of Western ontology, for Western ontology is primarily a dualistic ontology.

> Can we not find throughout our philosophy (and . . . theology) a . . . reverberation of a thought which could be called "positivist" (being exists, God exists by definition, if there has to be some thing, it could only be this world and this nature here, nothingness has no properties) and a "negativist" thought (the first truth is that of a doubt, what is certain first of all is a locus between being and nothingness, the model of infinity is my liberty, this world here is a pure fact) which inverts the signs and perspectives of the former, without eliminating or coinciding with it? Do we not find everywhere the double certitude that being exists, that appearances are only a manifestation and a restriction of being—and that these appearances are the canon of everything that we can understand by "being," that in this respect it is being in-itself which appears as an ungraspable phantom, an *Unding*? (*TFL* 89–90)

Merleau-Ponty critically claims that this dualism of being in itself and being for us leads to a "confusion in modern ideas of nature, man, and God" and to "equivocations in 'naturalism,' 'humanism,' and 'theism' " causing these attitudes to slide into one another (*TFL* 90). Yet he affirmatively claims that it is the job of philosophy to get beyond this dualism and describe how these attitudes or areas do slide into one another. Moreover, he claims philosophy is able to do this job only if being itself possesses regions which constantly move into one another and overlap (*TFL* 91).

Merleau-Ponty reports that he will try to uncover this overlapping, regional ontology by tracing recent developments in the natural and life sciences. He claims that recent science has uncovered many facts that do not fit into the outmoded Cartesian framework, yet that few scientists are willing to relinquish this framework. Philosophy must therefore trace the recent developments of science and draw the appropriate consequences for itself. Merleau-Ponty attempts this by first summarizing what he did in the previous course (just presented above). He briefly mentions the following. Physics raises questions that would free it from Laplacean models of a totally determined universe composed of individuals with absolute properties in external cause and effect relationships. Rather, physical entities are now to be conceived as "structures in an ensemble of operations," and determinism is to be conceived, not as the very connecting "tissue of the world," but, to say this metaphorically, only as a "crystallization on the surface of a 'cloud' (Eddington)" (*TFL* 91–92).

Merleau-Ponty considers whether these recent developments in science mark a return to idealism and quickly concludes with the following rhetorical question: "But if the concept of object is in dispute, how can critical idealism remain intact since it is entirely an analysis of the conditions and means of positing of an object?" (*TFL* 92). Merleau-Ponty further rejects idealism and proceeds to a positive expression of his own view of nature:

> What is called nature is certainly not a spirit at work in things whose aim is to resolve problems by "the most simple means"—but neither is it simply the projection of a power of . . . [our] thought . . . It is *that which makes there be,* simply, and at a single stroke such a coherent structure of a being, which we then laboriously express in speaking of a "space-time continuum" . . . Nature is that which establishes privileged states, the "dominant traits" . . . which we try to comprehend through the combination of concepts—nature is an ontological derivation, a pure "passage," which is neither the only nor the best one possible, which stands at the horizon of our thought as a fact which there can be no question of deducing. (*TFL* 93)

For Merleau-Ponty, then, we derive the concept of nature from the ontologically given—which is itself always in process. And yet this ontologically given is not derivable from anything else. It is simply given. It simply *is.* It is a brute fact that is revealed to us in stable or coherent structures of perception, in perceptions that are lived through and not the result of the classical metaphysics of the abstract idea or of mechanical cause and effect (*TFL* 93–94).

Merleau-Ponty now moves on to consider the life sciences and finds that they have also introduced many concepts in an effort to account for certain observed attributes of behavior but that no longer fit within the framework of classical ontology with its discretely defined regions. He says here that he has devoted several lectures to behavior at its different levels (*TFL* 94). It appears that he began these lectures, which he summarizes here, by analyzing lower-order behavior according to the notions of perceptual environment, work environment, and subject nature, introduced by J. von Uexull, and the notion of "behavior in internal circuits," discussed by E. S. Russell (*TFL* 94–95). In notions introduced by these authors he finds themes that confirm those that have long been present in his own writing. These themes may be enumerated as follows:

1. There is an interpenetration of the parts of an organism such that they define one another.
2. There is an interpenetration of the organism and its environment.
3. There is an interpenetration of the organism and other organisms, particularly with those of its own species. In addition, this lived coupling or empathy with another organism of its own species implies a sort of presignification, a sort of grasping of the sense or meaning of the behavior of another organism at a level prior to thought.
4. Behavior involves meaningful perceptual and work environments even in precognitive animal subjects.
5. Animal behavior is not just subject to a "push-causality" but is "directive"—yet directive in a way that does not involve the notion of entelechy.
6. Studies reveal that animals *see* and *show* themselves in ways that are not just the result of a static stimulus/response mechanism but that are general, and that therefore announce "the emergence of a symbolism whose 'comparative philology' (Lorenz) has yet to be constructed" (*TFL* 96).

All of the above display attributes that do not fit into the classical dualistic ontology that separates mind and matter into discrete regions and that breaks all things into discrete entities in external relationships of mechanical causality. All of the above display attributes that require an ontology of regions that slip into one another and overlap.

Merleau-Ponty also reports that he "tried to get at the nature of vital being by following the method of epistemology, that is to say, through reflection upon the knowledge of living creatures." Here the notions of " 'territory,' a working relation with its cohorts (Chauvin's study of migratory locusts) and finally a symbolic life (Firsch's study of language in bees)" were also analyzed (*TFL* 96–97). From these studies, at least according to Merleau-Ponty's judgment, "it emerged that all zoology assumes from our side a methodological *einfühlung* into animal behavior, with the participation of our perceptual life in animality" (*TFL* 97). Hence, here again we observe regions, this time regions of experience from different species, slipping into one another and overlapping.

This "species slippage" leads Merleau-Ponty to be critical of the neo-Darwinian adaptation principle of all or nothing. Under this principle it is assumed that if an organism has a certain attribute, it will survive; if it does not, it will not. Merleau-Ponty registers the following complaint:

> The result of this kind of thinking is to mask the most remarkable characteristics of living homeostases, namely, *invariance through fluctuation.* Whether we are dealing with organisms or animal societies, we do not find things subject to a law of all or nothing, but rather dynamic, unstable equilibria in which every rearrangement resumes already latent activities and transfigures them by decentering them. (*TFL* 97)

One of the consequences that we may draw from this dynamic adaptation, says Merleau-Ponty, is that we must abandon a hierarchical notion of evolution. Differences between species are qualitative (not just quantitative) and thus are lateral rather than strictly hierarchical (*TFL* 97).[1] In fact, we are able to witness all sorts of scattered developments and a wide variety of species adaptation, none of which fits neatly into a hierarchical schema. Also, Merleau-Ponty finds that the notion of "possibility" in animal behavior cannot be understood mechanistically as "another eventual occurrence," but must be grasped "as a general reality" for the species involved (*TFL* 98). Here again we see that the classical ontology of neatly separate regions and mechanical causality does not fit observed phenomena. A new ontology is called for that can make sense of overlapping regions and the gradual emergence of sense in animal life and perception.

Merleau-Ponty concludes these summary notes with the following statement:

> [W]e may already say that the ontology of life, as well as that of "physical nature," can only escape its troubles by resorting, apart from all artificialism, to brute being as revealed to us in our perceptual contact with the world. It is only within the perceived world that we can understand that all corporeality is already symbolism. (*TFL* 98)

The course Merleau-Ponty had planned for the following year was to trace "the emergence of symbolism in the transition to the level of the human body" (*TFL* 98). This course was postponed to allow Merleau-Ponty time to complete *The Visible and the Invisible.* (See *TFL* 99, note.) Yet he addresses the emergence of symbolism in the body in a later lecture course entitled "Nature and Logos: The Human Body," to which I now turn.

"Nature and Logos: The Human Body"

Merleau-Ponty here considers the works of A. E. Driesch because the problems Driesch encounters are typical of those encountered by contemporary embryology—problems which cannot be solved by a "philosophy of the object (mechanism and vitalism)" or by a "philosophy of the idea." These problems, Merleau-Ponty claims, can only be solved by a "philosophy of structure" (*TFL* 126). This is how he expresses it:

> The appearance of the notions of "gradient" and "fields"—that is to say, of "organo-formative" territories which impinge upon one another and possess a periphery beyond their focal region in which regulation is only probable—represents a mutation in biological thought as important as anything in physics. (*TFL* 126)

In other words, scientists working in the field of embryology are themselves uncovering phenomena that can be grasped by a nondualistic ontology of overlapping fields and structures, structures whose regulation is not autonomous and fixed but interactive and only probable. In addition, Merleau-Ponty once again mentions the neo-Darwinian theory of evolution and how developments in its empirical research no longer fit classical ontology. In particular he mentions that Darwinian scholars using the mutation-selection scheme increasingly recognize mutation and selection as parts of a whole, as linked structurally rather than as independent elements.

After a brief criticism of "idealist morphology" for attempting to reserve statistics as guiding ideas for the human mind and for abandoning "the interior of nature to inaccessible reality," Merleau-Ponty positively articulates his own view of evolution.

> A truly statistical conception of evolution would, on the contrary, attempt to define vital being starting from the phenomena; it would impose the principles of an "evolutionary kinetic" free from any schema of timeless causality or constraint from microphenomena, and would openly admit a scalar structure of reality, a plurality of "space-time levels." Organisms and types would then appear as "traps for fluctuations," as "patterned jumbles," as variants of a sort of "phenomenal" topology (F. Meyer), without any break with chemical, thermodynamic and cybernetic causation. (*TFL* 127–28)

For Merleau-Ponty, the way into evolutionary events is by a concrete phenomenological description that avoids an eternal causality on the one hand and microphenomena on the other. As he says in *The Structure of Behavior,* the phenomenal world is filled with perceptual gestalts, each ultimately connected to all the others as its field or ground. Yet the intuition of the perceiver can break the infinite reference of one gestalt to the other by grasping the situation's most meaningful whole (*SB* 139 ff.). The perceiver phenomenologically describes the patterned experience of other species, thus mapping out a topology of species. Members of the same species do not share a fixed, identical essence but are statistically similar, and, moreover, they are similar in many ways to members of other species. Furthermore, as we have seen, the phenomenological topology of species includes an attempt to grasp what *appears phenomenally* to those species. Here again we see Merleau-Ponty attempting to develop an ontology within which regions and species slip into one another and overlap. Here again, part of what he is saying is that humans have access to the lived field experienced by other animals only through human perceptual fields, and only by a decentering of these perceptual fields in order to try to accommodate and grasp the other.

One of the main reasons Merleau-Ponty has looked at evolutionary theory is to try to understand the advent of the human body. As we have just seen above, the means to do so is phenomenology, that is, through a lived perceptual encounter with the world of species development. He makes this very clear in the following statement:

> Furthermore (and this is the difference between phenomenology and idealism), life is not a simple *object* for a *consciousness.* In previous courses we have shown that life and external nature are unthinkable without reference to a perceived nature. Now we must think of the human body (and not "consciousness") as that which perceives nature which it also inhabits. Thus the relation between *Ineinander* which we thought we perceived can be recovered and confirmed. (*TFL* 128)

The slipping into one another (chiasm) of nature and the human body, and of the human body and perceptual consciousness can now be confirmed, according to Merleau-Ponty, and this will help us understand the *animation* of the human body, not as a vitalism or as the "miracle" of the production of consciousness out of a mechanistic nature, but as a slippage of perceived structures into one another.

This goal of understanding the animation of the human body demands, says Merleau-Ponty, "an 'esthesiology,' a study of the body as a perceiving animal" (*TFL* 128).

> For there can be no question of analyzing the fact of birth as if a body-instrument had received from elsewhere a thought-pilot, or inversely

> as if the object called the body had mysteriously produced consciousness out of itself. We are not dealing here with two natures, one subordinate to the other, but with a double nature. The themes of the *Unwelt,* of body schema, of perception as true mobility (*sichbewegen*), popularized in psychology and nerve physiology, all express the idea of corporeality as an entity with two faces or two "sides." Thus the body proper is a sensible and it is the "sensing"; it can be seen and it can see itself, and in this latter respect it comprises an aspect inaccessible to others, open in principle only to itself. The body proper embraces a philosophy of the flesh as the visibility of the invisible. (*TFL* 128–29)

Here we see Merleau-Ponty expressing in his lecture notes the philosophy of the flesh that is developed more fully in the partially completed chapters of *The Visible and the Invisible.* Since the body is both sensible and sensing, and since these attributes fold in on one another, they incorporate one another. The world is an extension of the body's flesh, as the body is an extension of the world's.

Here we also see Merleau-Ponty expressing part of what he means by the notion of the invisible. It is the other side (or inside) of the other sensible/sentient that I perceive from the outside. Since each sensible/sentient can only touch itself as likewise touching, see itself as likewise seeing, each maintains a privileged access only to itself; yet, because the properties of my corporeality can be extended to other human bodies, I have a certain access to them.

> If I am capable of feeling by a sort of interlocking of the body proper and the sensible, I am capable also of seeing and recognizing other bodies and other men. The schema of the body proper, since I am able to see myself, can be shared by all other bodies, which I can also see. (*TFL* 129)

Based on this observation, Merleau-Ponty now makes one of his most important claims: "The body schema is a lexicon of corporeality in general, a system of equivalences between the inside and the outside which prescribes from one to the other its fulfillment in the other" (*TFL* 129). Merleau-Ponty is here redefining the Cartesian consciousness of the private individual. Within his philosophy consciousness is perceptual consciousness, is a bodily openness unto the world with which it partially blends, and since as an embodied perceiver I perceive the world through a set of frameworks, a set of favored, habitual, and to a certain extent anonymous ways of doing things, these frameworks cease to be mine alone. These frameworks are formed where my perception meets and blends with the world and meets and blends with the frameworks of other gesturing corporeal subjects. As my hand touches, feels, palpates its surroundings, surroundings that fold back upon it, a set of equivalences is set up, allowing the body to feel the sleek or the rough of a surface. As my hand moves across a surface, as these movements send back to it a certain feel, a set of equivalences is set up, that is, the body adjusts its movements (its framework) to the sleek or rough surface (framework) it is caressing. The inside of the hand adjusts to the outside it is sensing and that folds back into it to be sensed, and it will be sensed as it is only if the body makes the proper adjustments. Thus the feel of the inside of the hand is articulated and fulfilled in the outside, as the outside is articulated and fulfilled in the inside. Moreover, because of the partial anonymity of the body, the set of equivalences that I develop between my body and the world flows into the sets of equivalences developed between the bodies of others and this same world. Thus, again, "the body schema is a lexicon of corporeality in general," the body schema is a framework of gestures aiming at a world that folds back upon it forming a meaning. This framework is a framework of meaningful gestures that can be understood in general, that can be applied to multiple circumstances, and that can be understood by all the members of the same species.

Merleau-Ponty now applies his understanding of the body/world relationship as mutual incorporation to Freud. "The theoretical concepts of Freudianism are corrected and affirmed once they are understood . . . in terms of corporeality taken as itself the search of the external in the internal and of the internal in the external, that is, as a global and universal power of incorporation" (*TFL* 129–30). Merleau-Ponty therefore sees the Freudian libido as a corporeal dimension, as a corporeal atmosphere or framework that cannot be escaped, since "nothing which is human is entirely incorporeal" (*TFL* 130). The sensuality of the body pervades all of its relationships to the world and others, for sensuality is the very means by which the body is related to all things.

Furthermore, since the unconscious is inconceivable as an unconscious *representation,* Merleau-Ponty redefines it as "feeling itself, since feeling is not the intellectual possession of 'what' is felt, but a dispossession of ourselves in favor of it, an opening toward that which we do not have to think in order that we may recognize it" (*TFL* 130). The unconscious is not something hidden beneath my consciousness but is out in front of it. It is an atmosphere or framework of my lived-through experience. (See *VI* 180, 189.) Moreover,

> [w]hen Freud presents the concept of repression . . . , it comprises a double movement of progress and regression, of openness toward the adult universe and of a relapse to the pregenital life, but henceforth called by its name, having become unconscious "homosexuality." Thus the repressed

> unconsciousness would be a secondary formation, contemporary with the formation of a system of perception—consciousness—and primordial unconsciousness would be a permissive being, the initial yes, the undividedness of feeling. (*TFL* 130–31)

Once again we see a sort of chiasm (an *Ineinander,* a flowing, slipping, or crossing into one another) expressed in Merleau-Ponty's thinking about the relationship between the unconscious and conscious awareness. The primordial unconscious is the undividedness of feeling at the level of prereflective, precognitive, pregenital childlike experience. This undividedness or unity or *sameness* with all corporeal beings is labeled as "homosexuality" in reflective, adult life—a label that folds back on the original experience that helps define it. This forms a relationship that M. C. Dillon refers to as a nonreciprocal reversibility, that is, the more primary term, here the original undividedness of primitive feeling, provides the bases for more reflective thought and language, which in turn folds back on the more primitive experience to help articulate it.[2] When Dillon makes this point he is speaking about the relationship between perception and language in Merleau-Ponty's philosophy. Yet Dillon's comments are relevant here, too, because Merleau-Ponty concludes this summary of his lecture notes by making the following claim:

> The preceding leads to the idea of the human body as a natural symbolism . . . We may ask what could be the relation between this tacit symbolism, or undividedness, and the artificial or conventional symbolism, which seems to be privileged, to open us toward ideal being and truth. (*TFL* 131)

Unfortunately, Merleau-Ponty disappoints us by saying that this topic will be dealt with in another series of courses—a series of courses that his untimely death abruptly precluded. Yet our despair can perhaps be at least somewhat abated, for Merleau-Ponty has left us other writings in which this task was at least provisionally undertaken, in particular the essays "Indirect Language and the Voices of Silence," "On the Phenomenology of Language," and several lectures in *Themes from the Lectures, 1952–1960.* I will turn to these writings in part 2, "The Invisible and *Logos,*" after a brief consideration of the notable essay "Eye and Mind."

4

Classical Ontology and Modern Ontology

"Eye and Mind"

"Eye and Mind," published just before Merleau-Ponty's death in 1961, was his most complete professional statement of his continually developing "later" philosophy. As Sartre has remarked: " 'Eye and Mind' . . . says it all, providing one can decipher it."[1] By carefully reading this work along with the rest of Merleau-Ponty's later texts, the keys to this deciphering are beginning to be placed in our hands.

Using the terminology of art history,[2] the primary concern of "Eye and Mind" may be expressed as a fundamental reevaluation of classical metaphysics and ontology, especially as represented by Descartes and Renaissance painters. By analyzing the modes of geometric representation that he finds in Descartes's work and in Renaissance painting, and by comparing them to the multifarious and elastic modes of representation of modern painters such as Cézanne, Klee, and Matisse, Merleau-Ponty makes the case for variable and open-ended forms of representation, and for a multifaceted and open-ended Being.

The brief exposition of "Eye and Mind" that I now proceed to offer follows Merleau-Ponty's five-section division.

1. This remarkable essay commences with a brief assessment of the instrumental form science had assumed by the middle of the twentieth century. This form of science, Merleau-Ponty claims, manipulates the world, and does so with great virtuosity, yet it gives up fully living in the world and fully encounters it only on rare occasions (*PrP* 159). Merleau-Ponty is thus cognizant and appreciative of the power of science to successfully manipulate the world using algorithms and operational definitions, though he cautions that we *must* "from time to time" place these instruments within the fuller context of *human* life as it is lived. If

this is not done, it is likely that human beings will also become the manipuladum of an instrumental formula, robbing us of our full humanity (*PrP* 160). Moreover, not only must science return to the lived "there is" of the world, but it must also return to this experience as an intersubjective phenomenon. Merleau-Ponty believes it is art, and especially painting, that draws upon this public and primordial openness upon being, "this brute fabric of meaning" (*PrP* 161). It is to painting that he here turns his attention.

2. Merleau-Ponty asserts that the painter paints with his or her body and not with his or her mind. Therefore, if we wish to understand the act of painting, we must begin with the painter's body—and this body must be conceived not as a physical object like any other but as a lived-through synergy of vision and movement. Since the human body is *actively* engaged in the world, all perception is intimately tied to its movement. The hand could not feel the sleek or the rough if it did not move across an object's surface. The eyes could not see if they did not move together to focus on the object seen. Yet, on the other hand, these movements would be blind if the visible did not fold back upon the means by which it is achieved. This lived overlapping or interweaving of vision and movement makes it impossible to conceive of vision as an operation of clear and distinct thought, as a "thought of seeing," as a representation. Vision is accomplished prereflectively by the body, not reflectively by thought (*PrP* 162).

Here Merleau-Ponty is once again articulating his reversibility thesis. Perception will never be fully clear to itself because it can never *completely* see itself seeing, for to see requires a movement that must be accomplished by the seer. The *seer* is therefore never fully seen, is never fully reflected upon, is always partially lost in the act. Correlatively, the seer is present to him or herself only in the act of perception, only by being perceptually present to the world. The human being, then, "is a self . . . through inherence of the one who sees in that which he sees" (*PrP* 163).

> This initial paradox cannot but produce others. Visible and mobile, my body is a thing among things; it is caught in the fabric of the world, and its cohesion is that of a thing. But because it moves itself and sees, it holds things in a circle around itself. Things are an annex or prolongation of itself; they are incrusted into its flesh, they are part of its full definition; the world is made of the same stuff as the body. This way of turning things around [*ces renversements*], these antinomies, are different ways of saying that vision happens among, or is caught in, things—in that place where something visible undertakes to see, becomes visible for itself by virtue

> of the sight of things; in that place where there persists, like the mother water in crystal, the undividedness [*l'indivision*] of the sensing and the sensed. (*PrP* 163)

It is thus in the body's lived-through encounter with the world that vision is born. Nature perceives itself by the human body (which is a natural body) folding back on itself and thus folding back upon the world. The human body, as we have seen Merleau-Ponty say, is a third kind of thing, neither a thing in itself nor a consciousness for itself (if Western tradition requires that we invoke these notions), but a lived-through blend of the two. The unity of the body therefore is not that of discrete parts in external relationship but that of a work of art whose parts are internally related in a way that is, nevertheless, different from the internal relations of pure ideas. Furthermore, "there is a human body when, between the seeing and the seen, between the touching and the touched, between one eye and the other, between hand and hand, a blending of some sort takes place—when the spark is lit between sensing and sensible" (*PrP* 163).

This "system of exchanges" between the sensing and the sensible explains all perception—and all painting, which of course is based upon it. And since all perception occurs in this exchange between the world and the body (which is made of the same stuff as the world), perception must occur in the body. It must somehow reproduce the thing on its inside. Yet this reproduction cannot be an intellectual reproduction; it is not a representation, it is not another "thing." It is like a painting, which we do not really see but see *according to*. Both perception and a painting open a visual experience, a visual expanse for the perceiver (*PrP* 164). In fact, "painting awakens and carries to its highest pitch a delirium which is vision itself, for to see is *to have at a distance*" (*PrP* 166). We have seen Merleau-Ponty develop this "to have at a distance" in great detail in *The Visible and the Invisible*. Perception cannot be complete coincidence with the perceived. For then perception would collapse into the perceived. Nor can perception be complete separation, for then there would be no contact at all. Either of these alternatives ends with the same result: no perception occurs. Merleau-Ponty's "to have and have not," this contact that remains distant, explains perception and has its roots in the two-dimensional structure of the body. The body sees and is seen, is in contact with itself as it separates from itself and opens upon the world. The painter, especially, manifests this splitting open of the body that allows the world to be present to the perceiver. "It is the mountain itself which from out there makes itself seen by the painter; it is the mountain that he interrogates with his gaze" (*PrP* 166). The world is on the outside, yet it somehow finds its equivalent on the inside of the human body. The painter probes and questions the visible about its appearance.

> What exactly does he ask of it? To unveil the means, visible and not otherwise, by which it makes itself a mountain before our eyes. Light, lighting, shadows, reflections, colors, all the objects of his quest are not altogether real objects; like ghosts, they have only visual existence. In fact, they exist only at the threshold of profane vision; they are not seen by everyone. The painter's gaze asks them what they do to suddenly cause something to be and to be *this* thing, what they do to compose this worldly talisman and make us see the visible. (*PrP* 166)

This questioning of the visible, Merleau-Ponty proceeds, is not the questioning by someone who knows of someone who does not. "The question comes from one who does not know, and it is addressed to a vision, a seeing, which knows everything and which we do not make, for it makes itself in us" (*PrP* 167). "The role of the painter is to grasp and project what is seen in him. The painter lives in fascination" (*PrP* 167).

Here Merleau-Ponty is clearly offering the painter as an example par excellence of perception as both *ek-stace* and chiasm. Perception, as we have witnessed throughout Merleau-Ponty's late texts, is the body's openness unto the world, is the body's aiming at a world outside itself, is the body's having at a distance. This occurs because the human body is a seer that is seen, a toucher that is touched—because perception occurs in the gap between them.

> We speak of "inspiration," and the word should be taken literally. There really is inspiration and expiration of Being, action and passion so slightly discernible that it becomes impossible to distinguish between what sees and what is seen, what paints, and what is painted. (*PrP* 167)

Once again we see here that it is the reversibility phenomenon that accounts for the birth of perceptual meaning. Here the painter's action is offered as a prime example of the flowing into one another of perception and the perceived, of the inspiration and expiration of Being. With a comment closing this section, Merleau-Ponty offers the painter's action as one last example of a perception that is not a "thought of seeing," that does not offer the world only as neatly presented within the geometrical perspective. "Essences and existence, imaginary and real, visible and invisible—a painting mixes up all our categories in laying out its oneiric universe of carnal essences, of effective likenesses, of mute meanings" (*PrP* 169). It is to an analysis of the classical perspective (the ontology of Descartes and others), which cannot tolerate the painter's open vision, that Merleau-Ponty turns next.

3. This "marvel of vision" (just described above) is precisely what Descartes attempts to circumvent. Rather than entering and living the full

field of vision with all of its imprecision, its confusions and its overlapping regions, Descartes seeks to intellectually understand how vision occurs. He seeks to intellectually construct it. The way Descartes attempts to do this is by the use of what he believes to be the apt comparison. He compares the action of light upon the eye to the action of things upon a blind man's cane. Action at a distance and the lived voluminosity of vision are removed at one stroke and vision is reduced to mechanical causality. Discrete things are placed in an empty objective space and in external relationships to one another. The human body and the eye are among these external things, thus reducing vision to the result of the geometrical relationships between these things and the eye. This cane metaphor leads Descartes to yet another comparison: vision is like an etching whose lines capture the external form of the thing but nothing more, whose lines reduce the voluminous visual field to three dimensions, and then to two and nothing more. An etching, then, does not resemble the world. "It 'excites our thought' to 'conceive,' as do signs and words 'which in no way resemble the things they signify' " (*PrP* 170–71). Thus Merleau-Ponty claims that for Descartes vision "is a thinking that deciphers strictly the signs given within the body" (*PrP* 171).

Merleau-Ponty offers an analysis of Descartes's comparison of vision to etchings:

> But what Descartes likes most in copper engravings is that they preserve the forms of objects . . . they present the object by its outside, or its envelope. If he had examined that other, deeper opening upon things given us by secondary qualities, especially colors, then—since there is no ordered or projective relationship between them and the true properties of things and since we understand their message all the same—he would have found himself faced with the problem of a conceptless opening upon things. (*PrP* 172)

Here again we see Merleau-Ponty suggesting that the body's lived-through contact with the world produces an open, voluminous vision/visible—an open vision/visible which nevertheless displays patterns, albeit spontaneous and open patterns. While Merleau-Ponty's philosophy of incarnate vision seeks to get at the open and spontaneous logos of the perceptual world, Descartes's philosophy seeks to intellectually construct vision from a few spatial (geometrical) indices—for, as we have seen and will continue to see below, even "depth is a third dimension derived from the other two" (*PrP* 172).

Merleau-Ponty here embarks upon an in-depth analysis of Descartes's conceptualization of depth as this third dimension—which according to Descartes we do not really see, which is a mere construction from the dimensions of width and height. If this is the case, surmises Merleau-Ponty, then space is either nothing or it is my presence to *all* space at once, that is, it is space without a point of view (*PrP* 172–73). For Descartes the following is true: "Orientation, polarity, envelopment are, in space, derived phenomena inextricably bound to my presence. *Space* remains absolutely in itself, everywhere equal to itself, homogeneous; its dimensions, for example, are interchangeable" (*PrP* 173). Descartes's treatment of space leads Merleau-Ponty to maintain that "like all classical ontologies, this one builds certain properties of beings into the structure of Being" (*PrP* 173). In other words, Descartes has taken one dimension of beings, that is, the exterior form of particular objects, or, even worse, one *human* technique (geometrical projection) for representing the properties of beings, and made it into the very structure of space and Being.

Even though Merleau-Ponty believes Descartes's move toward an abstract space was necessary to free ourselves from a blind adherence to contingency, he nevertheless believes Descartes's abstract space has severe limits. Moving beyond Descartes, we must attempt

> to understand that space does not have three dimensions as an animal has either three or two feet, and to understand that three dimensions are taken by different systems of measurement from a single dimensionality, a polymorphous Being, which justifies all without being fully expressed by any. Descartes was right in setting space free. His mistake was to erect it into a positive being, outside all points of view. (*PrP* 174)

Merleau-Ponty also thinks that Descartes was correct to borrow his view of space from the perspective painting of the Renaissance, for perspective painting allows for an agile representation of space. But again the error here is to take geometrical (or linear) perspective as *the* representation of space, to take a human technique for the structure of reality itself. More specifically, it was the theoreticians who "forgot the spherical visual field of the ancients." "But the painters, on the other hand, knew from experience that no technique of perspective is an exact solution and that there is no projection of the existing world which represents it in all aspects and deserves to become the fundamental law of painting" (*PrP* 174). Geometrical space does not give us space in itself, does not give us a God's eye view of space from nowhere, but refers us back to a human vantage point, and to one vantage point at that.

Continuing his analysis of the relationship between vision and thought in Descartes's philosophy, Merleau-Ponty finds that for Descartes "vision is conditioned by thought" and, conversely, that "the thinking that belongs to vision functions according to a program and a law which it has not given to itself. It does not possess its own premises, it is not a thought altogether present and actual; there is in its center a mystery of passivity" (*PrP* 175). This means that Descartes splits vision into two. On the one hand, there is the vision reflected upon and known only as conceived by thought and its principles. On the other hand, there is the vision that is enrolled in the body, that can only be grasped in the *act* of accomplishing it. Yet Merleau-Ponty concedes that "this de facto vision and the 'there is' which it contains" does not dilute Descartes's rationalist philosophy, since for Descartes both the existential "there is" (and the meaning and confusion that it supplies) *and* the light of reflective reason are grounded in God.

> We have to push Descartes this far to find in him something like a metaphysics of depth . . . God's being for us is an abyss. An anxious trembling quickly mastered; for Descartes it is just as vain to plumb that abyss as it is to think the space of the soul and the depth of the visible. Our very position, he would say, disqualifies us from looking into such things. Here is the Cartesian secret of equilibrium: a metaphysics which gives us decisive reasons to be no longer involved with metaphysics, which validates our evidences while limiting them, which opens up our thinking without rending it. (*PrP* 177)

Yet Merleau-Ponty claims that if Descartes found an equilibrium, one that involved a balance between philosophy and science, now this equilibrium seems to be lost forever. Science no longer accepts that its truths and models are derived from the existence and properties of God, and operational thought, as used in psychology, claims to explain the existential contact with oneself and the world that Descartes deemed unfathomable. Moreover, science no longer accepts Descartes's geometrical construction of reality. Operational thought will once again come into contact with philosophy only "when having introduced all sorts of notions which for Descartes would have arisen from confused thought—quality, scalar structure, solidarity of observer and observed—it will suddenly become aware that one cannot summarily speak of all these beings as constructs" (*PrP* 177).

Until this happens, Merleau-Ponty concludes, "nothing is left for our philosophy but to set out toward the prospection of the actual world. We *are* the compound of soul and body, and so there must be a thought of it" (*PrP* 177–78). Yet now we must no longer think of the human body in an instrumental way.

> Our organs are no longer instruments; on the contrary, our instruments are detachable organs. Space is no longer what it was in the *Dioptric,* a network of relations between objects such as would be seen by a witness to my vision or by a geometer looking over it and reconstructing it from outside. It is, rather, a space reckoned starting from me as the zero point or degree zero of spatiality. I do not see it according to its exterior envelope; I live in it from the inside; I am immersed in it. After all, the world is all around me, not in front of me. (*PrP* 178)

The immersion of ourselves in the lived compound of the soul and the body not only changes our conception of ourselves and space. It also dramatically changes how we are to conceive of light. "Light is viewed once more as action at a distance. It is no longer reduced to the action of contact or, in other words, conceived as it might be by those who do not see in it. Vision reassumes its fundamental power of showing forth more than itself" (*PrP* 178). Merleau-Ponty concludes by making what would be called, in the language of art historians, a modernist claim, and what would be called, in the language of contemporary philosophy, a postmodernist claim. "No more is it a question of speaking of space and light; the question is to make space and light, which are there, speak to us. There is no end to this question, since the vision to which it addresses itself is itself a question. The inquiries we believed closed have been reopened" (*PrP* 178). Vision is no longer the precise vision of geometry. It is a vision that is itself a probing, a palpation, a vision that reveals a sense but that also always remains open, voluminous.

4. Merleau-Ponty opens this section with a rather bold claim: "The entire modern history of painting . . . has a metaphysical significance" (*PrP* 178). The metaphysical significance he refers to here is not that of a system of detached ideas. In fact, this is what he believes modern painting is trying to avoid. More specifically, it is trying to avoid the abstract, geometrical representation that takes itself to be *the* form of reality. This attempted avoidance can be witnessed in Cézanne's lifelong struggle with depth. Following Cézanne, once we no longer take depth as fully expressed by the Cartesian coordinate system and linear perspective, depth no longer needs to be expressed as the "third dimension," simply as a variation of height and width.

> In the first place, if it were a dimension, it would be the first one; there are forms and definite planes only if it is stipulated how far from me their different parts are. But a *first* dimension that contains all the others is no longer a dimension, at least in the ordinary sense of a certain relationship according to which we make measurements. Depth thus

> understood is, rather, the experience of reversibility of dimensions, of a global "locality"—everything in the same place at the same time, a locality from which height, width, and depth are abstracted, of a voluminosity we express in a word when we say that a thing is *there.* In search of depth Cézanne seeks this deflagration of Being. (*PrP* 180)

This attempt to paint our full experiential openness upon Being extends beyond depth, beyond the line to colors as well. Color becomes one of the keys to reality and not just a secondary dressing for the primary quality of form. Yet just as form is not the master key to the visible (as we have just seen above), neither is color.

> The painter's vision is not a view upon the *outside,* a merely "physical-optical" relation with the world. The world no longer stands before him through representation; rather it is the painter to whom the things of the world give birth by a sort of concentration or coming-to-itself of the visible. (*PrP* 181)

We see Merleau-Ponty explicitly stating the reversibility thesis here. Within lived experience, where subject and object, activity and passivity blend, here meaning is formed. Moreover, there is nothing behind this meaning that "causes it" or that can rationally construct it. (See "Nature" above.) It is a meaning formed in a spontaneous, concrete encounter with the world. Merleau-Ponty expresses this thesis here by commenting about how a line of poetry seems to *form itself* or how "sometimes Klee's colors seem to have been born slowly upon the canvas, to have emanated from primordial ground" (*PrP* 182).

Merleau-Ponty also offers the example of the artist who is accomplished in different media (painting and sculpture, for example) to make the case that "there is a system of equivalences, a logos of lines, of lighting, of color, of reliefs, of masses—a conceptless presentation of universal Being" (*PrP* 182). Modern painting is not about using *one* system of equivalences (Descartes's coordinate system or any other) to represent reality, but is about multiplying the systems of representation. The line itself, for example, can be used to represent the exterior envelope of space or an object (as the classical painters used it) but it can also be used to "render visible; it is the blueprint of a genesis of things. The beginning of the line's path establishes or installs a certain level or mode of the linear" (*PrP* 183).

This does not mean that the "prosaic," "geometrical" line and the "poetic," "ontological" line must remain mutually exclusive. "[The artist] may choose with Matisse . . . to put into a single line both the prosaic definition of the entity and the hidden operation which composes in it such softness or inertia and such force as are required to constitute it as a *nude,* as *face,* as *flower*" (*PrP* 184). After all, says Merleau-Ponty, "it was Matisse who taught us to see contours not in a 'physical-optical' way but rather as structural filaments, as axes of a corporeal system of activity and passivity" (*PrP* 184).

Just as modern painting has reinterpreted the line and how it represents, it has also reinterpreted the representation of movement. In both painting and sculpture movement is no longer represented by the actual position of the parts of the body to each other and to their surroundings. This is the movement captured by the photograph, a capturing that is a strange freezing of movement, a representation of movement that shows no movement. The painter or sculptor can represent parts of an animal body at different moments in the movement sequence, with one part at one moment of the sequence, another at the next moment, and so on. This places the parts in a relationship to each other that they would never normally take, yet the impression of the observer is clearly that of motion. From these lessons of modern art, from the reinterpretation of space, of form and line, of color and movement, Merleau-Ponty draws the following conclusion:

> Now perhaps we have a better sense of what is meant by that little verb "to see." Vision is not a certain mode of thought or presence to self; it is the means given me for being absent from myself, for being present at the fission of Being from the inside—the fission at whose termination, and not before, I come back to myself. (*PrP* 186)

This is an obvious attack on the classical interpretation of vision offered by Descartes and Renaissance painters, and it is the presentation of a new way of seeing. Vision is not to be interpreted as a reflective "thought of seeing," a reflective presence of self to self. Vision is a prereflective relationship to the world. The reflective presence of oneself to oneself occurs only mediated by this distance from oneself, by the ecstatic relationship toward the thing. Nor is vision to be conceived as geometrical projection, as the neat presentation of objects only by the projection of their geometrical form. Perception opens to a visual field that is a gestalt, that is an open system of shifting patterns. Yet these patterns bear a meaning—something Merleau-Ponty thinks painters have always been aware of.

> Painters always knew this. Da Vinci invoked a "pictorial science" which does not speak with words (and still less with numbers) but with *oeuvres* which exist in the visible just as natural things do and which nevertheless

> communicate through those things "to all the generations of the universe." This silent science, says Rilke (apropos of Rodin), brings into the *oeuvre* the forms of things "whose seal has not been broken"; it comes from the eye and addresses itself to the eye. We must understand the eye as the "window of the soul." "The eye . . . through which the beauty of the universe is revealed to our contemplation is of such excellence that whoever should resign himself to losing it would deprive himself of the knowledge of all the works of nature, the sight of which makes the soul live happily in its body's prison, thanks to the eyes which show him the infinite variety of creation; whoever loses them abandons his soul in a dark prison where all hope of once more seeing the sun, the light of the universe, must vanish." The eye accomplishes the prodigious work of opening the soul to what is not soul—the joyous realm of things and their god, the sun. (*PrP* 186)

In a very real sense, then, Merleau-Ponty is attempting, with modern painters, to move beyond the classical (geometrical, Cartesian) interpretation of perception. In the language of philosophy rather than that of art history, Merleau-Ponty is clearly moving beyond modernism but not quite into what is currently being labeled postmodernism. Unlike most postmodernists who disavow any connection with a perception that carries its own meaning and for whom language carries all meaning, Merleau-Ponty clearly finds a visual field replete with meanings—even if these meanings are not fully clear or "rational" in themselves. He further confirms our contact with the visible world.

> A Cartesian can believe that the existing world is not visible . . . A painter cannot grant that our openness to the world is illusory or indirect, that what we see is not the world itself, or that the mind has to do only with its thoughts or with another mind. He accepts with all its difficulties the myth of the windows of the soul: it must be that what has no place is subjected to a body—even more, that what has no place be initiated by the body to all the others and to nature. We must take literally what vision teaches us: namely, that through it we come into contact with the sun and the stars, that we are everywhere all at once, and that even our power to imagine ourselves elsewhere . . . borrows from vision and employs means we owe to it. (*PrP* 186–87)

> "The visual quale" gives me, and alone gives me, the presence of what is not me, of what is simply and fully. It does so because, like texture, it is the concretion of a universal visibility, of a unique space which separates and reunites, which sustains every cohesion. . . . Every visual something,

> as individual as it is, functions also as a dimension, because it gives itself as the result of a dehiscence of Being. (*PrP* 187)

In "Eye and Mind," as well as elsewhere, we have seen Merleau-Ponty discuss how a visual something—a line or a color—can also function as a dimension. Just as the yellow of indoor light quickly becomes the dimension within which or by which we perceive the objects it illuminates, so also a line ceases to be the mere exterior envelope of an object and becomes its means of revealing its very meaning and being. The dehiscence or splitting open of Being that Merleau-Ponty is referring to here is revealed in the fact that the line is not prosaic, it is lyrical, it is dimensional, it carries a meaning, refers beyond itself. The line is able to do this, is able to represent Being this way because Being itself is revealed this way, with implied, even invisible elements. Merleau-Ponty puts it this way: "What this [dimensionality of the visible] ultimately means is that the proper essence [*le propre*] of the visible is to have a layer [*doublure*] of invisibility in the strict sense, which it makes present as a certain absence" (*PrP* 187). In fact, "vision encounters, as at a crossroads, all the aspects of Being" (*PrP* 188). Vision encounters form, color, and even the implied, the invisible, that which helps reveal a being as a dimension, as something, as the bearer of a meaning.

This meaning is only formed, as Merleau-Ponty has stated throughout, in the incarnate subject's active encounter with the world. "This precession of what is upon that one sees and makes seen, of what one sees and makes seen upon what is—this is vision itself" (*PrP* 188). Furthermore, "there is no break at all in this circuit; it is impossible to say that nature ends here and that man or expression starts here. It is, therefore, mute Being which itself comes to show forth its own meaning" (*PrP* 188).

5. Merleau-Ponty opens this short concluding section with a brief summary statement of his analysis of the relationship between art and Being.

> Because depth, color, line, movement, contour, physiognomy are all branches of Being and because each one can sway all the rest, there are no separated, distinct "problems" in painting, no really opposed paths, no partial "solutions," no cumulative progress, no irretrievable options. (*PrP* 188)

From the modern painter, then, we learn of the richness, the fullness, the voluminosity of Being. We learn that it is multidimensional, that these dimensions themselves are organic and shifting, that they influence and penetrate one another, that they cannot be accounted for apart from the embodied perceiver, and that the human representation of them is abstract, inexact, and incomplete. Moreover, just as painting is limited in its ability to represent Being, so is the language of science, philosophy, and literature. Merleau-Ponty's position here represents a decidedly frontal attack on, in the language of art history, the classical view, and in the language of contemporary philosophy, the modernist view inherited from Descartes and others. It is an attack on the view that claims that Being is fixed and reducible to a few abstract indices. Yet the loss of this view should not lead to regret, for the loss of absolutes is not the loss of all knowledge, as it seems to be for many postmodernists. We may not know Being or nature in its full positive density, but we do have some sense of what is not true, what does not work—in art, science, and life. Since artistic and intellectual syntheses are temporal and therefore continue to unfold, with new information changing the syntheses, artistic and intellectual syntheses are never complete. Yet since these human and therefore embodied syntheses open upon Being in a similar (though not identical) way, they will all communicate with each other, at least in some lateral way, and the very first opens the possibility of inexhaustible variation (*PrP* 188–90).

PART 2

''THE INVISIBLE AND *LOGOS* ''

5

"The Invisible and *Logos*"

Part 2 of *The Visible and the Invisible,* "The Invisible and *Logos,*" was undoubtedly intended to discuss speech, language, and the move from the mute perceptual idea to the abstract idea of language. Evidence for this claim can be found by observing the way the terms *invisible* and *logos* are used in the "Working Notes" and in chapter 4, "The Intertwining—the Chiasm." Consider the following from the "Working Notes":

> Meaning is *invisible,* but the invisible is not the contradictory of the visible: the visible itself has an invisible inner framework (*membrure*), and the in-visible is the secret counterpart of the visible, it appears only within it, it is the *Nichturprasentierbar* which is presented to me as such within the world—one cannot see it there and every effort to *see it there* makes it disappear, but it is *in the line* of the visible, it is its virtual focus, it is inscribed within it (in filigree). (*VI* 215)

We have already seen that for Merleau-Ponty, where the active, lived-through body meets the patterned structures of the world, there meaning is formed. The structures of the world fold in upon the body, just as the body's favored frameworks fold back upon the world. In fact, the framework for experience is created in this lived interaction. In this lived interaction, meaningful perceptual gestalt structures are formed. These structures are experienced as an articulated foreground against a background or horizon of less focused support. The background structures are necessary and help bring the foreground into focus, yet they themselves remain implied. They are, we now see, the "invisible" lines of force that help bring meaning into play but that themselves remain hidden. It is these invisible gestalt frameworks that line the perceived, that allow it to be what it is. (See also *VI* 171.)

We saw above in the analysis of "The Intertwining—the Chiasm" that Merleau-Ponty was just beginning to analyze the relationship between this perceptual gestalt or idea and the abstract ideas of language. For Merleau-Ponty, the transition from one to the other is to be accomplished by the body, for if perception is already a meaningful bodily organization of the perceptual field, then perception is already a gesture, is already expression. This perceptual expression slips (*Ineinander*) into the vocal expression called speech, which in turn is the basis for the more abstract written expressions of language. The perceptual idea, then, is sublimated into the abstract ideas of language by means of the bodily gesture called speech. Thus, broadly speaking, what Merleau-Ponty means by the *invisible* is the idea, the implied lining or structure of both perception and language, and what he means by *logos* is expression, at first as mute perception, then as spoken gesture, then as abstract literature. (See *VI* 208.) Moreover, the invisible structures of the mute perceptual idea or the abstract idea of language fold in upon and fuse with their means of expression. The entire structure of the perceptual gestalt, including the "invisible" lines of force that run from the horizon to the foreground, is its logos, its structure, its expression, its meaning. The invisible is the idea, the interior lining of *expression,* both perceptual and linguistic, that helps provide its structure or sense or logos. (See also *VI* 170–71.) Under the heading of "The Invisible and *Logos*" I have therefore collected Merleau-Ponty's late lectures and essays on perception and its relation to expression and language. It is to these that I now turn, beginning with the lecture notes and proceeding to the published essays.

The Sensible World and the World of Expression

Merleau-Ponty opens this lecture summary with the claim that while his contemporaries recognize what is original in perceptual consciousness, they attempt to explain it in terms of abstract thought and judgment. This, according to Merleau-Ponty, is unfortunate because he believes that familiarity with perception "makes possible a new analysis of the understanding" (*TFL* 3). In other courses Merleau-Ponty will eventually proceed to a new analysis of language and understanding. Here he offers a description of the original structure of perception:

> For the meaning of a perceived object when picked out from all others still does not stand isolated from the constellation in which it appears; it is articulated only as a certain *distance* in relation to the order of space, time, motion, and signification in general in which we are established. The meaning of the object is given only as a systematic deformation of our universe of experience, without our being able to name its operative

principle. Every perception is a perception of something solely by way of being at the same time the relative imperception of a horizon or background which it implies but does not thematize. Perceptual consciousness is therefore indirect or even inverted in relation to an ideal of adequation which it presumes but never encounters directly. (*TFL* 3–4)

With these comments on the gestalt character of perception in place, Merleau-Ponty proceeds to draw the following conclusion: "Thus if we understand the perceived world as an open field, it would be just as absurd to reduce everything else to this as to impose upon it a 'universe of ideas' which owed nothing to it" (*TFL* 4). According to this characterization of the perceived, it is just as impossible to reduce language and thought to perception as it is to reduce perception to language and thought. In his typical dialectical fashion he states the following:

There is truly a reversal when one passes from the sensible world, in which we are caught, to a world of expression, where we seek to capture significations to serve our purpose, although this reversal and the "retrogressive movement" of the truth are solicited by a perceptual anticipation. Properly speaking, the expression which language makes possible resumes and amplifies another expression which is revealed in the "archaeology" of the perceived world. (*TFL* 4)

It is clear from the above passage, and particularly from the last sentence, that for Merleau-Ponty, perceptual meaning is prolonged and sublimated by language, which fixes meanings that fold back on the perceived world. Dillon's phrase "nonreciprocal reversibility" captures well here Merleau-Ponty's intent. Perceptual expression is prolonged by linguistic expression which folds back upon perception to help express it—but "this retrogressive movement" is itself solicited by the more primary perception.

Merleau-Ponty's lecture summary proceeds to offer a report of a study of motion as an example of this reversibility phenomenon articulated above. He reports that the unity of the human body, or rather, that the unity of the bodily gesture, is projected into visual experience just as the visual is introjected into the framework of the body. This projection and introjection happens simultaneously and with a partial blending of each with the other. The specific study that Merleau-Ponty cites tells of two points of light that are flashed in succession onto a screen. The observer of this phenomenon does not perceive two discrete points of light but "traces of a single movement" (*TFL* 5).

Here what happens is that external forces insert themselves into a system of equivalents that is ready to function and in which they operate upon

> us, like signs in a language, not by arousing their uniquely correspondent signification but, like mileposts, in a process which is still unfolding, or as though they were picking out a path which . . . inspired them at a distance. (*TFL* 5–6)

In addition to confirming the ongoing dialectical exchange between the structures of the embodied and engaged perceiver and the structures of the perceived, Merleau-Ponty's analysis of this experiment leads him to draw the following important conclusion: "Thus perception is already expression. But this natural language does not isolate; it does not 'bring out' what is expressed, but allows it to adhere in its own way more to the 'perceptual chain' than to the 'verbal chain' " (*TFL* 6). "Natural language," then, expresses the meaning where it is, *in* the perceptual chain. As we have just seen, movement is offered as an example of this "natural language," for "movement is inscribed in the texture of the shapes or qualities and is . . . the revelation of their being" (*TFL* 6). Movement reveals a *meaning* that is embedded in perception and that is not constituted by language.

Continuing his analysis, Merleau-Ponty claims that we cannot really understand this perceptual meaning without taking account of the body subject and studies of the body schema. "In these studies the body is the seat of a certain praxis, the point from which there is something to do in the world, the register in which we are inscribed and whose inscription we continue" (*TFL* 7). Another way of saying this is that the body is the seat of certain norms, certain favored ways of being-in-the-world, certain habitual ways of performing tasks within it. These norms reveal a complex relationship between the knowledge of space and the movement of the body.

> On the one hand, gnosis is founded upon praxis, since the elementary notions of point, surface, and contour in the last analysis only have meaning for a subject modified by locality and himself situated in the space in which he unfolds the spectacle of a point of view. (*TFL* 8)

> On the other hand, gnosic space is relatively independent of the practical expression of space, as is evident from pathological cases where serious practical impairments are compatible with ability to handle spatial symbols. The relative autonomy of super structures which outlast the practical conditions which generated them—or at least for a time hides their collapse—permits us to say with equal truth that we are conscious because we are mobile or that we are mobile because we are conscious. Consciousness, in the sense of knowledge, and movement, in the sense

> of displacement in objective space, are two abstract moments of a living structure which can very well extend its limits but would also destroy its powers if it were to abolish those limits. (*TFL* 8)

Merleau-Ponty, always the consummate dialectician, expresses here, with a dialectical suitability few have accomplished, his view that all the parts of human experience cohere in an experiential whole. And even though the limits of this experiential whole can be expanded, by adding various abstract structures to it, they cannot be destroyed without the loss of meaning. To paraphrase Kant, abstract structures would be empty without the lived experience, and the experience would be blind or directionless without the strictures of higher forms of consciousness. Of course, this is not to mistake Merleau-Ponty as a sort of Kantian, at least in the sense of possessing a priori forms of consciousness. For Merleau-Ponty, the body is oriented toward the world by means of lived-through bodily structures, but these are structures in the making. As the body practically interprets the world through meaningful frameworks, the world folds back on these frameworks, constantly changing them and readjusting them.[1]

Merleau-Ponty concludes this lecture summary with the claim that insofar as psychologists "locate praxis and recognize it as an original domain, they are in position to understand the strict relations between mobility and all the symbolic functions as well as to renew our conception of understanding" (*TFL* 8). He continues: "The body is the vehicle of an indefinite number of symbolic systems whose intrinsic development definitely surpasses the signification in 'natural' gestures, but would collapse if ever the body ceases to prompt their operation and install them in the world and our life" (*TFL* 9). The lived experience of active, incarnate subjects can be sublimated but not destroyed, at least not destroyed without the collapse of the symbolic systems built upon it.

Here we have seen Merleau-Ponty provide a description of the original gestalt structure of perception, briefly and provisionally describe the relationship between the natural symbolism of perception and the cultural symbolism of language as a nonreciprocal reversibility, and outline the mobile body as the seat of an indefinite number of open-ended symbolic systems. In the next course, he will turn his attention more specifically to cultural and literary expression.

Studies in the Literary Uses of Language

Language is often studied as it has already been formed, claims Merleau-Ponty, and this unfortunately leaves aside the creation of new linguistic meanings, achieved, for example, by the writer taking up already established expressions and making them say something new. One of the paradoxes of expression is how the writer can express his or her life as it is lived and yet can do so only by elaborating this life in a language that cuts or severs the writer from "the living community." This paradox (as well as others) has caused many authors to ask a series of questions about the practice of writing and the theories of language. It is in the context of these sorts of questions that Merleau-Ponty will confront the work of Valéry and Stendhal.

Beginning with Valéry, Merleau-Ponty informs us that Valéry at first has a great mistrust of the communicative power of language and that he "wrote only for himself," yet his skepticism is soon overcome in theory and practice because language is simply there; it is there in effective human use.

> Moreover, there was at least one form of language which one could not reject precisely because it did not pretend *to say something*—namely, poetry. Now, upon examination it became clear that the reason why poetry does not convey signification by effacing itself before what it says, like a plain statement, . . . is because it always has more than one signification. Thus, it was necessary to admit, at least in the case of poetry, the "miracle" of a "mystical union" of sound and meaning . . . But once this prodigy has been discovered in poetry in the strict sense, it can be found again in "that endlessly active poetry which torments static language, opening or narrowing the meaning of words." (*TFL* 15–16)

From this claim Merleau-Ponty proceeds to inform us that Valéry draws the following conclusion:

> These variations in language, which at first appear to support the skeptic, are ultimately the proof of its meanings, since words would not change in meaning unless they were trying to say something. The justification of poetry rehabilitates the whole of language, and in the end Valéry admits that even the intellectual is not a pure consciousness . . . , and that our clarity comes from our commerce with the world and with others. (*TFL* 16)

What then does Merleau-Ponty think is valuable in Valéry's work? We may answer the following: Valéry abandons skepticism with respect to language. Language is everywhere in human use and is everywhere used successfully. And even where it is not used successfully, the fact that it continues to be used indicates that it is trying to say *something,* and this something has its roots in our lived-through encounter with others and the world.

With a few brief comments on Stendhal, Merleau-Ponty informs us that Stendhal's main problem as a writer, by his own admission, is the inability "to feel" and to be *aware* as a writer at the same time. Yet ultimately Stendhal resolves this difficulty, for, "out of the first person" and the ease with which the ego can slip "into any role," "he creates the means of an entirely new art" (*TFL* 17). Thus what Merleau-Ponty finds agreeable in Stendhal is that which fits his own framework of the embodied subject. Just as for Stendhal, the use of the first person gains access to any human role, for Merleau-Ponty the body subject opens out to and fuses with certain general structures of natural and social being. The idea of an embodied self in chiasm with the natural, social, and linguistic is something Merleau-Ponty will turn his attention to in his next course.

The Problem of Speech

Merleau-Ponty opens this summary of lecture notes with the claim that for Saussure speech does not simply express an already constituted language. In fact, a *conscious speaker* is needed to take up language, to sustain it, and, in so doing, this speaker is in the position to modify language.

Merleau-Ponty here briefly discusses the typical distinction between sign and signification, something he spent a great deal of time dealing with and rejecting in *Phenomenology of Perception*. Both traditional empiricism and rationalism claim that words are more or less empty shells for things already perceived (or represented) or for thoughts already conceived. As Merleau-Ponty says in *Phenomenology of Perception*, "we refute both intellectualism and empiricism by simply saying that the word has a meaning" (*PhP* 177). First of all, he argues that the empiricists treat language as a third-person process described from the outside, that they do not account for the speaking subject who must engage a categorial attitude in order to use language fully. Second, he argues against the rationalists by claiming that the naming of an object does not follow a separate intellectual recognition but is that recognition itself. The aware linguistic naming of the object is the recognition of the object. There is, then, no clear distinction between signification and sign, between meaning already formed (empirically or rationally) and the vehicle of linguistic signification. Signification and sign are largely interdependent.

Here in the lecture summary Merleau-Ponty makes the same point by appealing to Saussure's challenge of the rigid distinction between sign and signification. Especially in speech, where sound and meaning fold in upon one another, sign and signification must be seen as internally linked. In fact, sound and meaning can only be related by a conscious speaker.

> The well-known definition of the sign as "diacritical, oppositive, and negative" means that language is present in the speaking subject as a system of intervals between signs and significations, and that, as a unity, the act of speech simultaneously operates the differentiation of these two orders. (*TFL* 20)

Merleau-Ponty goes on to say that "the purpose of this course is to illustrate and to extend the Saussurean conception of speech as a positive and dominating function" (*TFL* 20). He does so first by appealing to Saussure's idea of the acquisition of language. Roman Jakobson, a follower of Saussure, distinguished "between the mere factual presence of a sound or phoneme in the child's babbling and the proper linguistic possession of the same element as a means of signifying" (*TFL* 20). The latter, of course, requires that the child be *aware* enough to integrate the sound of his or her speech into the accepted patterns of the surrounding language. This Merleau-Ponty agrees with. Yet when Jakobson analyzes this phenomenon he appeals to an abstract judgment, which itself, as Merleau-Ponty reminds us, relies upon language. Merleau-Ponty insists on the need to take the conscious speaker into account in order to understand language, yet this conscious speaker is not yet the reflective, judgmental subject. Rather, there is a consciousness of speech that occurs *in* its lived act.

Merleau-Ponty next cites the studies that link the acquisition of language to emotional development and warns us to avoid a single, linear causality when attempting to understand language and speech.

> The relations with others, intelligence, and language cannot be set out in a lineal and causal series: they belong to those cross-currents where *someone lives.* Speech, said Michelet, is our mother speaking. Thus while speech puts the child in a more profound relation to she who names every thing and puts being into words, it also translates this relation into a more general idea. (*TFL* 21)

Merleau-Ponty thus focuses on the totalities of the child's lived relations to the world and others, for thought and language develop within the context of this totality—and in fact they are a part of it.

Merleau-Ponty turns to the works of Kurt Goldstein to further confirm the Saussurean notion of the primary role of speech. Goldstein at first distinguishes between automatic, external language and "language in the full sense . . . , which is related to a categorial attitude" (*TFL* 22). In Goldstein's later "works, however, these two orders are related so that there is no longer signification on the one hand and the 'instrumentalities' of language on the other. In the long run, the instrumentalities of language only remain functional as long as the categorial attitude is intact and, universally, the impairment of instrumentalities compromises the grasp of significations" (*TFL* 22–23). Seeing that signification and the instruments of language are intimately related, Merleau-Ponty is led to the following conclusion:

> There is thus a sort of spirit of language, a spirit always freighted with language. For language is the system of differentiations through which the individual articulates his relation to the world . . . The Saussurean notion of the diacritical sign [is] . . . interrelated and akin to Humboldt's idea of language as a "perspective on the world." (*TFL* 23)

For Merleau-Ponty, then, the differential structure of language must be seen to be in relationship with the individual's aware openness into the world. This is confirmed by what Merleau-Ponty says about the painter, the musician, and the author.

> Just as the painter and the musician make use of the objects, colors, and sounds in order to reveal the relations between the elements of the world in a living unity . . . so the writer takes everyday language and makes it deliver the prelogical participation of landscapes, dwellings, localities, and gestures, of men among themselves and with us. In literature, the ideas, as in music and painting, are not "the ideas of the intellect," they are never quite detached from what the author sees . . . For this reason, the writer's work is a work of language rather than of "thought." His task is to produce a system of signs whose internal articulation reproduces the contours of experience. (*TFL* 24–25)

Reading this last sentence leads one to believe that language simply articulates the contours of lived experience. Yet Merleau-Ponty quickly goes on to claim that the relationship between language and experience is more complex. It is circular, as we have already seen. Language folds back on the sense world to help articulate it, but it is a linguistic structure that is itself called forth by the perceptual. Merleau-Ponty says of Proust that "no one has better expressed the vicious circle or prodigy of speech, that to speak or to write is truly to translate an experience which, without the word that inspires, would not become text" (*TFL* 26), and quotes him directly:

> The book of unknown signs within me (signs in relief it seemed, for my attention, as it explored my unconscious in its search, struck against them, circled around them like a diver sounding) no one could help me read by any rule, for its reading consists in an act of creation in which no one can collaborate. (Marcel Proust, *A la recherche du temps perdu,* II, 23; quoted by Merleau-Ponty in *TFL* 26)

Once again what we see both Proust and Merleau-Ponty expressing here is the idea of a nonreciprocal reversibility, for lived perceptual relationships are prolonged by a language which folds back upon the perceptual to help articulate it in ever new ways. Yet, as creative as language is, one can see here in Merleau-Ponty's lecture summaries that the primary term is still lived-through bodily perception, for the linguistic expression itself, even if not determined, is solicited by the more primordial perception.

Merleau-Ponty closes this summary with the following claim: "These descriptions of the inchoate, regressive, and sublimated forms of speech should enable us to study its relation in principle to instituted language and to clarify the nature of institution as the act of birth of all possible speech. This will be the topic of another course" (*TFL* 26). As John O'Neill notes (*TFL* 26), the reference here to a future course is probably to "Institution in Personal and Public History." It is to this lecture that I now turn.

"Institution in Personal and Public History"

In this important course Merleau-Ponty will use the concept of institution (introduced by Hegel) to correct the concept of constitution that is used by what he refers to as the philosophy of consciousness (undoubtedly a reference to the type of philosophy developed by Descartes, Kant, and perhaps Husserl). For this philosophy of consciousness, he says, "there are only objects which [consciousness] has itself constituted" (*TFL* 39). Objects, other human beings, and even its own past are present to consciousness only if they are constituted by consciousness.

We have already seen Merleau-Ponty claim that for the philosophy of consciousness even the concept of time is constituted by consciousness. Temporality, that is, the present gradually sliding into the past and toward the future, is itself spread out before a reflective, intellectual subject and is thus constituted by an act of consciousness. Merleau-Ponty does agree, as has already been mentioned, that time must be present to the subject, otherwise time would not pass. Yet he argues that time runs beyond the subject, otherwise the subject would constitute time, which subsequently would not pass, for it would be spread out spatially before the reflective subject and would therefore be fully present. The subject does not create time but must be a part of it, must exist within its flow. The subject then is not primarily the reflective intellectual consciousness outside of time which constitutes all meaning, even that of time. The conscious temporal subject is influenced by events, yet simultaneously influences them. In fact, meaning and structure are formed where the incarnate subject and worldly event come together. The conscious subject is then able to take up this structure or framework and use it to interpret future events.

This structural notion of the subject enables Merleau-Ponty to make the following claim about the subject's relationship to his or her own past. "What I have begun at certain decisive moments would exist neither far off in the past as an objective memory nor be present like a memory revised, but really between the two as the field of my becoming during that period" (*TFL* 40). Just as the subject's relationship to the world can be characterized as an *ek-stace,* as a stretching out of itself toward a natural horizon that runs beyond it yet with which it remains in contact, so also the subject's relationship to his or her own past can be characterized as an *ek-stace,* as a spread, as a stretching out of the present moment toward a past with which the present remains in contact. This means of course that just as the present remains in contact with the past, the past remains in contact with the present.

> Thus what we understand by the concept of institution are those events in experience which endow it with durable dimensions, in relation to which a whole series of other experiences will acquire meaning, not as survivals or residues, but as the invitation to a sequel, the necessity of a future. (*TFL* 40–41)

Certain structures of past experience are therefore instituted, are carried forward in the incarnate subject and become the means by which present and future events are interpreted.

Merleau-Ponty illustrates this concept of institution in a number of ways, for he believes that it *exists* in a number of different ways. He believes, for instance, that something like the experience of institution occurs at the level of animal behavior. He cites the phenomenon of impregnation (whereby an animal is imprinted with the first living being that it sees) to support this claim, since all future relationships will be conditioned by this initial imprint. There is also a sort of impregnation at the biological level of human experience, for the conflicting emotions that the child feels toward his or her mother or father (the Oedipal and Electra conflicts) can carry into adult relationships and infuse them with meaning. Yet something new occurs at the level of mature adult life.

> [For] . . . in man the past is able not only to orient the future or to furnish the frame of reference for the problems of the adult person, but beyond that to give rise to an elaboration: in this case conservation and transcendence are more profound, so that it becomes impossible to explain behavior in terms of the past, anymore than in terms of its future. (*TFL* 41)

Not only does the past orient the present and the future, but the present and future fold back upon the past to continually reorient it. In adult life, there are many cases of "this crystallization upon each other of the past and the future, of subject and object, of positive and negative"—whereby earlier experiences provide frameworks for future events which continue to transform them (*TFL* 42). This crystallization of the past, present, and future upon each other occurs with the development of ideas and knowledge as well, for even in mathematics "the series of 'idealizations' which reveals the whole number as a special case of a more essential number does not land us in an intelligible world from which it might be deduced; rather it resumes the evidence proper to the whole number, which remains understood" (*TFL* 42). In other words, past and present ideas orient the development of future ideas, and future ideas develop by an elaboration of ideas already present, yet they enlighten them in ways that were not originally present. Moreover, if ideas are influenced by the historical process, perhaps, conversely, history can be guided or even dominated by principle. Yet Merleau-Ponty warns us against this move, for principles are not ubiquitous and situations must be understood laterally (*TFL* 43–44). That is to say, I grasp my situation through its concrete structure and by placing it in relief, by reflectively comparing it to other situations—which in turn I understand, although never completely, through my own situation. Since no two things, events, situations, or people are ever exactly the same, universal concepts are limited, partial, and grasp only similarities or resemblances. Yet perhaps these similarities or resemblances are enough for human knowledge.

> There occurs a simultaneous decentering and recentering of the elements in our personal life, a movement by us toward the past and of the reanimated past toward us. Now this working of the past against the

> present does not culminate in a closed universal history or a complete system of all the possible human combinations with respect to such an institution as, for example, kinship. Rather, it produces a table of diverse, complex probabilities, always bound to local circumstances, weighted with a coefficient of facticity, and such that we can never say of one that it is more true than another, although we can say that one is more false, more artificial, and less open to a future in turn less rich. (*TFL* 44)

For Merleau-Ponty, then, human knowledge is situated in concrete conditions and in a history in which the past continues to influence the present and future, just as they fold back to continually reinterpret the past. Since knowledge systems are historical in this manner, they continue to transform themselves. And since knowledge systems are formed by historically contingent and engaged individuals, they remain partial, provisional, and never complete. Within Merleau-Ponty's philosophy the lack of completeness and absoluteness do not preclude knowledge. They may preclude an absolute standard by which we may positively compare particular human solutions, but they do not preclude the possibility of judging which solutions have not worked.

Merleau-Ponty concludes this series of illustrations and comments with the announcement that they were "intended as a revision of Hegelianism, which is the discovery of phenomenology, of the living, real and original relation between the elements of the world" (*TFL* 44). He goes on to state, however, that the problem with Hegelianism is that it subjects the phenomenon to the totalizing rational vision of the philosopher. As we have seen above, Merleau-Ponty's phenomenology is not to submit to the constructions of a rationalist philosophy. Phenomenology must not claim to rationally *constitute* being in the present. It is to mediate being; it is to describe it in its temporal unfolding, and it is to describe it as it continually unfolds. In this case phenomenology becomes fundamental ontology and even a metaphysics of history (*TFL* 44–45).

The Problem of Passivity: Sleep, the Unconscious, Memory

There are only a few points that need to be highlighted in this section, points which deepen those made by Merleau-Ponty in the previous section about the historical character of human experience. His comments here on passivity in human experience are worth our attention.

> [I]t is possible to speak of passivity only on the condition that "to be conscious" does not mean "to give a meaning" . . . which one projects

> onto an ungraspable object of knowledge, but to realize a certain distance, a certain variation in a field of existence already instituted, which is always behind us and whose weight . . . only intervenes in the actions by which we transform it. For man, to live is not simply to be constantly conferring meaning upon things but to continue a vortex of experience which was set up at our birth at the point of contact between the "outside" and he who is called to live it. (*TFL* 47)

As we have seen several times, within Merleau-Ponty's philosophy, the incarnate, needful subject does not simply passively receive information from the world. The body subject acts into the world with needs, desires, and interests, and receives information from it only within the context of these needs, desires, and interests. Where the needful body meets the world, there meaning is formed. This meaning is created neither by a nature in itself mechanically impacting upon a passive subject nor by the subject's active, intellectual construction. Human meaning is partially created by an incarnate subject who is thrown into a natural and social world, into a spatial and temporal horizon that precedes the subject, which the subject takes up and, in fact, is a certain variation of. The incarnate subject takes up the results of this meaningful encounter with the temporal social and natural world and carries it forward. Merleau-Ponty's position is thus able to suggest a more adequate way to approach the relationship between past and present, activity and passivity.

> Only if we abandon the description of the problem in terms of "representation" can we reconcile the immanence and transcendence of the past, the activity and passivity of memory. Instead of a "representation" (*Vorstellung*), we might begin by viewing the present as a certain unique position of the index of being-in-the-world, and our relations with the present when the present slips into the past, like our relations with our surroundings, might be attributed to a postural schema which unfolds and shapes a series of positions and temporal possibilities, so that the body could be regarded as that which answers each time to the question "where am I and what time is it?" (*TFL* 51)

As was indicated above, within Merleau-Ponty's philosophy time cannot be accounted for without the embodied subject, for without this subject there would be no experience of the passing of time, only an eternal now. Yet time must run beyond or transcend the subject, otherwise time would be spread out spatially before the reflective subject as a representation. It would be fully *present* to the subject, and therefore would not pass. As Merleau-Ponty expresses it here, the way to understand the relationship between the past and present is not by way of an intellectually introduced representation but by the incarnate subject's aware being-in-the-world. The incarnate subject is *ek-stace,* is thrown into the world, is a lived relationship to the world, not a reflective turning in on itself. This, according to Merleau-Ponty, is the best way to grasp the relationship between the present and past. The present moment of lived experience is a leaping out of itself toward the past. It is an experiential, lived-through contact, whereby the present stretches from where it is to that which is beyond it. It is therefore through this lived embodied experience that we are able to ask properly and begin to answer the questions "where am I?" and "what time is it?"

Husserl at the Limits of Phenomenology

In this remarkable course on the notions of ideality and historicity in Husserl's late writings, we find Merleau-Ponty once again focusing on and presenting Husserlian themes he is in fundamental agreement with. Merleau-Ponty investigates two of Husserl's late texts, "Die Frage nach dem Ursprung der Geometrie als intentional-historisches Problem" (which later appeared in *Die Krisis der europäischen Wissenschaften und die transzendentale Phanomenologie,* 1962; *The Crisis of European Sciences and Transcendental Phenomenology,* 1970)[2] and "Umsturz der kopernikanischen Lehre" (which remains unpublished).[3] From the first text, Merleau-Ponty extrapolates and presents the following ideas (most of which he incorporates into his own later philosophy of the flesh). First, ideality and historicity have a common source, and this source must be placed between a timeless realm of ideas and the flow of discontinuous events. It must be placed in a third dimension which would be "the genesis of ideality"—which we will see explicated below. Second, each stage of knowledge (ideality) contains more than its expressed or manifest ideas. "Each stage opens up a field and prepares themes which their author can only see as an outline of what is to come (*Urstiftung*), but which, when *handed down* (*tradiert*) to succeeding generations along with the earliest advances, become useful through a sort of second creation (*Nachstiftung*)" (*TFL* 115). In other words, as implied outlines get handed down, along with their origins, succeeding generations begin to take them up and use them in new ways—thus opening new pathways of knowledge.

How are we to understand this generation of thought from past possessions? If there were a timeless realm of ideality, how could these ideal significations possibly enter individual consciousness? Or, contrarily, if we start, "as we must," says Merleau-Ponty, with the birth of these ideas within us, how can we move to the generation of their ideal existence, their existence for *any* mind? The answer to the question is that it is only by way of speech that a sense or meaning can be detached from an individual consciousness and become available for any mind. Summarizing Husserl's thought, Merleau-Ponty expresses this point in the following way:

> But language is "interwoven" (*Verflochten*) with our horizon upon the world and humanity. Language is borne by our relation to the world and to others, yet language in turn supports and creates it. It is through language that our horizon is open and endless (*endlos*) and it is because we know that "everything has a name" that each thing exists and has a way of existing for us. (*TFL* 117–18; translation slightly altered)

This passage is of interest because we see here in Husserl the *Ineinander* (the flowing into one another) of language and one's openness upon the world and others. Just as the world's solidity is sublimated in language, the stabilizing influence of language folds back upon the flow of our experience of the world to help solidify it. Thus we see here in Husserl the expression of an experience that is very close to the chiasm between perception and language that we have seen Merleau-Ponty develop in his later works. What is important to see here is that it is language that helps free significations from the individual's experience and makes them exist in themselves. But this "making public" of an individual signification must still be accounted for. And it is the phenomenon of *Ineinander* or chiasm that can once again help to provide this account.

> Before anything else within my sphere of consciousness there is a sort of message from myself to myself: I can be sure today of thinking the same thought that I thought yesterday because the wake which it leaves is or could be retraced exactly by a fresh act of productive thought, which is the only veritable fulfillment of my recollected thought. I think in this near past, or rather yesterday's thought passes into today's thought: there is an encroachment of the passive upon the active which is reciprocal. (*TFL* 118)

As we have just seen above, it is the folding of experience into speech and speech into experience that helps provide the unity of thought within the individual, for speech helps identify and stabilize significations, yet speech could not do this if there were not some prior connection of experiences in the incarnate subject's lived-through temporal experience. If past ideas and memories did not connect within experience, if one moment of experience simply dropped off with no connection to the others, experience would be impossible. Or at least a continuous experience would be impossible, for each moment of experience would simply be a flash of awareness with no connection to any other. Language alone cannot connect experiences, cannot create the continuity of experience. Language helps stabilize and pull together meanings, but it does so only by folding back upon the temporal field of lived-through experience.

Yet speech does assist this stabilizing process and is able to help accomplish even more, for it assists with the movement of significations from one individual to another.

> Speech passes from the sphere of one consciousness to another by the same phenomenon of encroachment or propagation. As a speaking and active subject, I encroach upon the other who is listening, as the understanding and passive subject I allow the other to encroach upon me. Within myself and in the exercise of language I experience activity in every case as the other side of passivity. And it is thus that ideality "makes its entrance" (*Eintritt*). (*TFL* 118–19)

Ideality is formed not by a passive reception of worldly impressions, of a past memory, or of another's thought. It is formed by an active awareness turning back upon these experiences at the same time that it is carried forward by them. Speech assists or, even more, is a part of this process, for it helps actively carry meanings from the world, the past, and others at the same time that these fold upon it and help carry it. If it is true that speech is interwoven with our experience of the world, the past, and others, then there is no realm of pure ideality separate from speech.

> No more in my relationship to myself than in my relationship to others is there any question of survey or of pure ideality. There is, however, the recuperation of a passivity by an activity: that is how I think within the other person and how I talk with myself. Speech is not a product of my active thought, standing in a secondary relation to it. It is my practice, my way of working, my "*Funktion*," my destiny. Every production of the mind is a response and an appeal, a coproduction. (*TFL* 119, translation slightly altered)

Thus for Merleau-Ponty every production of speech is a coproduction of past and present, of passive and active, of self and other, of self and community, and of self and history. The speaker actively meets the past, the world, and others, fuses with them, and carries them forward.

Yet the analysis of speech and ideality is still not complete, for it seems that ideality exists independent of speech and even independent of humanity, for ideas continue to exist even when people are asleep or even when they are no longer living.

> However, this does not place ideal being outside of speech, but merely obliges us to introduce an essential mutation in speech, namely, the appearance of writing. It is writing which once and for all translates the meaning of spoken words into ideal being, at the same time transforming human sociability, in as much as writing is "virtual" communication, the speaking of x to x which is not carried by any living subject and belongs in principle to everyone, evoking a total speech. (*TFL* 119)

It is written language, then, that accounts for the ideal existence of meaning, the existence of meaning beyond the time during which it was lived and spoken, yet it is a written language that would remain dead if it were not continually taken up and renewed by living subjects.

All these Husserlian examples of *Ineinander* found in the relationships between the past and the present, between the passive and the active, between self and world, openness unto the world and others—all these, as we have seen, Merleau-Ponty incorporates into his own philosophy of flesh and chiasm.

These same notions of openness that Merleau-Ponty finds in Husserl at the superstructural level of language and culture, he also finds in Husserl's discussion of the base structure in "Umsturz der kopernikanischen Lehre." Here Husserl claims that the Copernican view regards nature as *only* an object. Merleau-Ponty summarizes Husserl's thought as follows:

> Through meditation we must again learn of a mode of being whose conception we have lost, the being of the "ground" (*Boden*), and that of the earth first of all—the earth where we live, that which is this side of rest and movement, being the ground from which all rest and all movement are separated, which is not made of *Körper,* being the "source" from which they are drawn through division, which has no "place," being that which surrounds all place, which lifts all particular beings out of nothingness, as Noah's Ark preserved the living creatures from the Flood. (*TFL* 121–22)

This notion of the world as an open-ended horizon or ground is something that we have seen Merleau-Ponty incorporate into both his philosophy of nature and his philosophy of the flesh. He also finds in Husserl's work notions that get very close to his own idea of intercorporeality. He finds in Husserl the expression of a kinship between the lived world and the lived body, between the lived body and the bodies of others, between the lived body and the bodies of worldly objects. All this is lost (or rather forgotten) within the Copernican framework, for everything is perceived from the point of view of a detached observer who treats everything as a pure in itself. But this view cannot provide its own foundation, for it treats all perception as the result of external events, yet somehow (we know not how) places its own view outside of the framework of these events. We must therefore return to the view of the world as an open environment, within which the perceiver is already enveloped. It is this view, along with others, that Merleau-Ponty develops with great subtlety in his late works.

To summarize, we have seen Merleau-Ponty express the following ideas in the Collège de France lecture notes. Perception expresses an original structure of meaning that cannot be explained by either abstract thought or by an atomistic, mechanistic, reductionistic materialism. The relationship between this natural symbolism and the cultural symbolism of language can best be understood as a nonreciprocal reversibility, with perception as the more primary term. Moreover, we saw that the body is to be characterized as the seat for the development of an indefinite number of symbolic systems.

We saw that skepticism with respect to the expressive power of language was abandoned because language is everywhere in use and is everywhere used successfully. In addition, since it keeps trying to say something, and to say something with greater and greater accuracy, there must be something to say. This something has its roots in the individual's lived encounter with the world and others. We also saw that first-person experiences can be used to gain access to the experiences possessed by other human beings because the embodied subject opens out to and fuses with certain general structures of the natural and social worlds. In fact, there is a chiasm between the structures of the embodied self on the one hand and the structures of the natural, social, and linguistic on the other.

We saw that speech does not simply express an already constituted language. Rather, a conscious speaker is needed to take up language to sustain and modify it. There is no neat distinction between signification and sign, between meaning already formed (either empirically or rationally) and the vehicle of language. Sign and signification are codependent, sign and signification, sound and meaning fold in upon one another. Therefore, using language means consciously grasping meaning. This happens in the act of speech, which has a positive and central role to play in language. The diacritical structure of language must then be seen to fold back upon the life-world, upon the individual's aware openness to and partial fusion with the world and others. Thus, a relationship of nonreciprocal reversibility exists between the life-world and speech, with life-world as the more primary term. (See also *VI* 170.)

We also saw that the notion of institution is to be used to correct the concept of constitution. The subject is not primarily the reflective subject that intellectually constructs all meaning. The subject is primarily the lived bodily subject that opens out to, that stretches out to the world, others, and the past from where it is centered in the body. The self is an experiential/structural self formed only in relationships. The self takes up these relationships, carries them forward and reintegrates them (without grasping the whole) as new information is added to them. We saw that many of the concepts formed here around this idea of institution were "intended as a revision of Hegelianism, which is the discovery of phenomenology, of the living, real and original relation between the elements of the world" (*TFL* 44). Phenomenology is to mediate being; it is to help bring being to expression. Yet it is primarily to describe and not rationally construct this unfolding of being.

And finally, we saw that the notions of ideality and historicity have a common origin somewhere between a timeless realm of ideas and the contingent flow of events. We are to understand the historical generation of thought not by appeal to an eternal realm of ideas. Thought comes to birth within human beings and nowhere else. Hence, it is only by way of speech that meanings can be detached from the individual's consciousness and become available as ideals for all other minds. Language is interwoven with the world and others. It is borne by them but, in turn, helps carry them, with the lived relation to the world and others as the more primary term. It is thus language which helps create and communicate ideality, yet it is a language that folds back on the perceived world that helped inspire it.

Most of the linguistic themes discussed in the lecture notes just investigated appear in the 1952 essays "On the Phenomenology of Language" and "Indirect Language and the Voices of Silence," both of which were republished in *Signs* in 1960. The benefit of the essays is that they are professional articles fully expressing the author's integrated thought rather than brief summaries of lecture notes covering a range of topics. I will here present Merleau-Ponty's ideas on language as they appear in both of these essays. My presentation will follow the section headings and/or numbers of the English editions of these published articles.

"On the Phenomenology of Language"

Husserl and the Problem of Language

According to Merleau-Ponty, the early Husserl (in *Logical Investigations* [*Logische Untersuchungen,* 2 vols., 1900–1]) develops an eidetic of language, whereby the essence of language is intellectually constructed as an object before reflective consciousness. Specific empirical languages are then seen by Husserl as a manifestation of this eidetic ideal.

For the later Husserl, as Merleau-Ponty interprets him, "language appears as an original way of intending certain objects, as thought's body ([*Formal and Transcendental Logic;*] *Formale und transzendentale Logik,* 1929) or even as the operation through which private thoughts acquire intersubjective value and, ultimately, ideal existence ([*Origin of Geometry;*] *Ursprung der Geometrie,* 1939)" (*Signs* 84–85).

Merleau-Ponty proceeds to cite Pos who, emphasizing the later Husserl, defines the phenomenology of language as contact with the speaking subject and with the unity of language which cannot be grasped when studied by the scientist as a collection of fortuitous objective events (*Signs* 85).

The Phenomenon of Language

Within the context of Husserl's early and late philosophy of language, Merleau-Ponty proceeds to discuss four points.

Language and Speech

It is not possible to simply juxtapose the two views of language that are characterized by Husserl and others, that is, language as an object and language as a subject. Yet this is also what Saussure attempts to do with his theory of language, *language* (*langue*) as it appears diachronically (as an object for the scientist); and his theory of *speech* (*parole*), language as it appears synchronically (for a speaking subject). Saussure reasoned that it is impossible to reduce one of these views to the other "because," says Merleau-Ponty, "a panchronic view would inevitably blot out the originality of the present," a notion which Saussure regarded as untenable (*Signs* 86). Pos also limits himself to alternately describing objective language and the experience of speech. But, Merleau-Ponty argues, even in Pos's case phenomenology simply becomes psychological description added to the objective truths of linguistics—just as the teacher adds a description of the student's *experience of learning* to the already established truths of mathematics. Yet Merleau-Ponty claims that it is precisely *this* that is impossible. What is needed is a dialectical view that, rather than simply juxtaposing, *integrates* these two views of language. It is to this integration that Merleau-Ponty turns his attention.

What he finds is that "at first the 'subjective' point of view envelops the 'objective' point of view; synchrony envelops diachrony," for every past view was once present, and past views are incorporated into the present as a meaningful and unified system (*Signs* 86). Yet synchrony is also enveloped by diachrony because fortuitous elements continually make their way into the system. This, says Merleau-Ponty, presents us with a double task: (1) we must not only understand language as a *presently* unified system, but also as "a moving equilibrium," and (2) since the equilibrium is *moving,* we must realize that the linguistic system "never exists wholly in act but always involves latent or incubating changes" (*Signs* 87).

To understand language as a moving equilibrium, "we must recognize that the present diffuses into the past to the extent that the past has been present" (*Signs* 87). We have seen Merleau-Ponty deal with temporality and sedimentation in the lecture notes. We have seen that just as the past influences the present, the lived-through present opens upon a past with which it has remained in contact and that it continues to reorient. Just as the past orients the present system, the present system reorients the past. They flow into one another. "History," then, "is the history of successive synchronies, and the contingency of the linguistic past invades even the synchronic system" (*Signs* 87).

Moving now to take up the second point that language "never exists wholly in act," Merleau-Ponty claims the following:

> [The linguistic system] is never composed of absolutely univocal meanings which can be made completely explicit beneath the gaze of a transparent constituting consciousness. It will be a question not of a system of forms of signification clearly articulated in terms of one another . . . but of a cohesive whole of convergent linguistic gestures, each of which will be defined less by a signification than by a use value. (*Signs* 87)

The linguistic system, then, must be taken as a whole, for each word has a meaning only in use, only in the act of speech and writing which must draw upon the whole of language. Moreover, these meanings can never be arranged before and fixed by reflective consciousness, for reflective consciousness itself requires language to think.

With additional comments directed against Husserl's early reflective eidetic of language and toward a positive expression of his own view, Merleau-Ponty now proceeds to assert what has to be one of the earliest expressions of multiculturalism.

> Far from particular languages appearing as the "confused" realization of certain ideal and universal forms of signification, the possibility of such a synthesis becomes problematical. If universality is attained, it will not be through a universal language which would go back prior to the diversity of language to provide us with the foundations of all possible language. It will be through an oblique passage from a given language that I speak and that initiates me into the phenomenon of expression, to another given language that I learn to speak and that affects the act of expression according to a completely different style—the two languages (and ultimately all given languages) being contingently comparable only at the outcome of this passage and only as signifying wholes, without our being able to recognize in them the common elements of a single categorial structure. (*Signs* 87)

Two points should be emphasized here. First, we understand speech only by confronting it and taking it up as aware subjects, only by, at least initially, coming into experiential contact with it. Second, understanding this act of speech gives us at least some access to the lived speech acts of others. Since humans have similar bodies (not identical bodies—for there is no ideal essence here, either of the human body or of language) that open to the world in similar ways, we have the opportunity to at least glimpse the experience of others. We have the opportunity to form what we have seen Merleau-Ponty refer to as the lateral universal—eschewing the ideal essence of Husserl and the "universal" of much of Western philosophy.

Merleau-Ponty concludes here that phenomenology is not at all merely a *psychological* description of the individual's incorporation of the objective structures of language that are already determined by linguistic scientists. Rather, phenomenology teaches us something new. It teaches us that we must abandon the idea of the eidetic character of language, of an ideal, universal language that preexists actual languages. As Merleau-Ponty expresses it, "It teaches me a new conception of the being of language, which is now logic in contingency—an oriented system which nevertheless always elaborates random factors, taking what was fortuitous up again into a meaningful whole—incarnate logic" (*Signs* 88). Language is a system that continually reorients itself by attempting to meaningfully integrate the contingent events that continually confront it. Language is a dialectical integration of the synchronic and diachronic, of the subjective and objective.

The Quasi-Corporeality of the Signifying

In this section Merleau-Ponty argues, as he did in the lecture notes, that language *does* say something. Yet it is able to do so not because each word refers singly to its own meaning. Accepting Saussure's view of language that signs refer laterally to other signs, he nevertheless believes (contrary to Saussure and, currently, to Derrida) that signs, taken as a gestalt whole, refer beyond themselves to significations. This means that each sign expresses something only by reference to a certain framework of linguistic implements. Yet even with the linguistic equipment taken as a whole, there is still no simple relationship or correspondence between signs and already composed significations.

> [O]nce the act of speaking is acquired it presupposes no comparison between what I want to express and the means of expression I make use of. The words and turns of phrase needed to bring my significative intention to expression recommend themselves to me, when I am speaking, only by what Humboldt called *inner Sprachform* . . . that is, only by a certain style of speaking from which they arise and according to which they are organized without my having to represent them to myself. There is a languagely meaning of language which effects the mediation between my as yet unspeaking intention and words . . . Organized signs have their immanent meaning, which does not arise from the "I think" but from the "I am able to." (*Signs* 88)

Here again we see the idea of language as a self-orienting system. It is not simply a voice for already clearly conceived significations, but helps form those significations from within. It is in the lived act of speaking, the aware, lived act of using language that words and meanings suggest themselves to the speaker. Language bears these meanings, just as these meanings fold back upon language to help organize it.

Merleau-Ponty proceeds even further to compare this ability of language to pull significations together to the human body's ability to organize its perceptual field.

> I have a rigorous awareness of the bearing of my gestures or of the spatiality of my body which allows me to maintain relationships with the world without thematically representing to myself the objects I am going to grasp or the relationships of size between my body and the avenues offered to me by the world. On the condition that I do not reflect expressly upon it, my consciousness of my body immediately signifies a certain landscape about me, that of my fingers a certain fibrous or grainy style of the object. It is in the same fashion that the spoken word (the one I utter or the one I hear) is pregnant with a meaning which can be read in the very texture of the linguistic gesture (to the point that a hesitation, an alteration of the voice, or the choice of a certain syntax suffices to modify it), and yet is

> never contained in that gesture, every expression always appearing to me as a trace, no idea being given to me except in transparency, and every attempt to close our hand on the thought which dwells in the spoken word leaving only a bit of verbal material in our fingers. (*Signs* 89)

The comparison between bodily gestures and linguistic gestures is so compelling that Merleau-Ponty is able to say that the actions of language to pull significations together "are eminent cases of corporeal intentionality" (*Signs* 89). Just as the lived act of my body has a certain hold on the world that makes it meaningful for me, the lived act of speech, itself a bodily gesture, has a certain hold on a field of significations that organizes them in a useful and meaningful way.

The Relationship of the Signifying and the Signified: Sedimentation

Speech is comparable to bodily gesture, then, because speech is in the same relationship to its meaning as a gesture is to its goal. Speech aims at or intends a meaning. Yet the comparison can be made even more exact:

> My corporeal intending of the objects of my surroundings is implicit and presupposes no thematization or "representation" of my body or milieu. Signification arouses speech as the world arouses my body—by a mute presence which awakens my intentions without deploying itself before them. (*Signs* 89)

Merleau-Ponty is again suggesting that just as lived-through bodily actions do not need to intellectually represent objects, the body, or their relationships to each other to be successful, so the lived acts of speech do not need to reflectively represent words or their relationships to each other to be meaningful. As I speak rapidly or listen to a quickly delivered speech, I do not intellectually represent words or reflectively consider each signification. Yet both remain meaningful to me and other listeners.

Here, in the act of speech, the significative intention is nothing but "a *determinate gap* to be filled by words" (*Signs* 89). Yet these significative intentions do not yet exist as determinate thoughts. Language does not translate already existent thought. It helps form it. "For the speaking subject, to express is to become aware of; he does not express just for others, but also to know himself what he intends" (*Signs* 90). And, as has already been stated, the speaking subject is able to fully form a significative intention only by using the available instruments of language. Merleau-Ponty gives eloquent expression to this point, which I cite to bring this section to a close.

> The significative intention gives itself a body and shows itself by looking for an equivalent in the system of available significations represented by the language I speak and the whole of the writings and culture I inherit. For that speechless want, the significative intention, it is a matter of realizing a certain arrangement of already signifying instruments or already speaking significations (morphological, syntactical, and lexical instruments, literary *genres,* types of narrative, modes of presenting events, etc.) which arouses in the hearer the presentiment of a new and different signification, and which inversely (in the speaker or the writer) manages to anchor this original signification in the already available ones. (*Signs* 90)

Consequences for Phenomenological Philosophy

In this last section, as its title indicates, Merleau-Ponty considers what consequences the preceding descriptions of language will have for phenomenological philosophy. It seems that in Husserl, the relationship between phenomenology and philosophy is not clear, for while he regards phenomenology as only preparatory for the crowning achievement of an independent philosophy, his insistence on beginning with life-world descriptions means that something of these descriptions remains in his philosophy of universal constitution (*Signs* 92). Merleau-Ponty reflects on this inconsistency and comments that

> [t]he reason why the return to the *Lebenswelt* (and particularly the return from objectified language to speech) is considered absolutely necessary is that philosophy must reflect upon the object's mode of presence to the subject—upon the conception of the object and of the subject as they appear to the phenomenological revelation—instead of replacing them by the object's relationship to the subject as an idealistic philosophy of total reflection conceives of it. From this point on, phenomenology envelops philosophy, which cannot be purely and simply added on to it. (*Signs* 92–93)

For Merleau-Ponty, phenomenology must focus on the prereflective lived-through activity of the incarnate subject, on the actual mode of presence of worldly objects, others, and language to the experiencing incarnate subject. By doing so, abstract thought may be considered a sublimation of the concrete encounter with the world rather than being conceived as an exemplification of a prior eidetic ideal. The phenomenology of language especially makes clear the relationship between phenomenological descriptions and the abstract thought of philosophy, for the description of language makes clear that language helps form thought—including philosophical thought. There can really be no abstract philosophical thought outside of language that would come to control or dominate language.

> If speech is what we have said it is, how could there possibly be an ideation which allows us to dominate this *praxis?* How could the phenomenology of speech possibly help being a philosophy of speech as well? And how could there possibly be any place for a subsequent elucidation of a higher degree? It is absolutely necessary to underline the *philosophical* import of the return to speech. (*Signs* 93)

Yet perhaps these descriptions of speech, lived gesture, and the lived-through body in general can simply be regarded as psychological descriptions, for after all, the body and its relationships to the world (including language and its relationships to thought) are still grasped by a pure reflecting consciousness (at least as conceived by Husserl). Yet as Merleau-Ponty says, expressing this point in the first person,

> [I cannot] classify the phenomenon of incarnation simply as psychological appearance, and if I were tempted to do so, I would be blocked by my perception of others. For more clearly (*but not differently*) in my experience of others than in my experience of speech or the perceived world, I inevitably grasp my body as a *spontaneity which teaches me what I could not know in any other way except through it.* Positing another person as an other myself is not as a matter of fact possible if it is *consciousness* which must do it. To be conscious is to constitute, so that I cannot be conscious of another person, since that would involve constituting him as constituting, and as constituting in respect of the very act through which I constitute him. (*Signs* 93–94)

Husserl is acutely aware of this problem but never resolves it. Rather, since it appears to be overcome in actual experience, since each *I* appears to live with the contradiction of another constituting subject that it constitutes, the problem is overcome by simply being ignored. But rather than passing over this contradiction, Merleau-Ponty embraces it:

> This subject which experiences itself as constituted at the moment it functions as constituting is my body. We remember that Husserl ended up basing my perception of a way of behaving (*Gebaren*) which appears in the space surrounding me upon what he calls the "mating phenomenon" and "intentional transgression." (*Signs* 94)
>
> Everything happens as if the functions of intentionality and the intentional object were paradoxically interchanged. The scene invites me to become

> its adequate viewer, as if a different mind than my own suddenly came to dwell in my body, or rather as if my mind were drawn out there and emigrated into the scene it was in the process of setting for itself. I am snapped up by a second myself outside me; I perceive an other. (*Signs* 94)

Merleau-Ponty proceeds to claim that speech must certainly be considered a prime example of this reversibility phenomenon. It is a prime example of "'ways of behaving' which reverse my ordinary relationship to objects and give certain ones of them the value of subjects. And if objectification makes no sense in respect to the living body (mine or another's), the incarnation of what I call its thinking in its total speech must also be considered an ultimate phenomenon" (*Signs* 94). Since at the level of concrete experience the relationships between incarnate self and world, incarnate self and others, are both characterized by the phenomenon of chiasm (of reversibility, of *Ineinander,* of flowing into one another), then there can be no objectification of these experiences, for reflecting consciousness cannot place itself outside of these phenomena in order to construct them.

Yet if this is the case, we may draw the following conclusion:

> In a sense, phenomenology is all or nothing. That order of instructive spontaneity—the body's "I am able to," the "intentional transgression" which gives us others, the "speech" which gives us the idea of an ideal or absolute signification—cannot be subsequently placed under the jurisdiction of an acosmic and a pancosmic consciousness without becoming meaningless again. It must teach me to comprehend what no constituting consciousness can know—my involvement in a "pre-constituted" world. (*Signs* 94–95)

Phenomenology must be an existential phenomenology, for nothing can teach me about the world, others, and my past other than my actual engagement with them. And of course Merleau-Ponty is here making the same claim about language. The only way I know it is by actually using it. The only way that it is made manifest is as one of the ways of behaving that reverses the relationship between subject and object, one of the ways of behaving that is *Ineinander,* a flowing into one another of speaking and listening, of signifying and signified. Furthermore, "[i]f the phenomenon of language is in fact the common act of the signifying and the signified, we would deprive it of its distinctive characteristic by realizing the result of expressive operations in advance in a heaven of ideas" (*Signs* 95). These ideas would already be formed and therefore nothing new would be expressed by language.

> In any case the place of truth would still be that anticipation (*Vorhabe*) through which each spoken word or acquired truth opens a field of understanding, and the symmetrical recovery (*Nachvollzug*) through which we bring this advent of understanding or this commerce with others to a conclusion and contract them into a new view. (*Signs* 95)

Merleau-Ponty's discussions of Husserl and the temporality of experience that we witnessed in the lectures at the Collège de France are instructive here. We observed that there was no separation between passivity and activity, and that this *Ineinander* or chiasm was manifested in the relationship between the body and the world, between past and present, between incarnate self and others and between language and all of these experiences. Just as the body receives information from the world, it acts into and organizes it. Just as the past is carried into the present, the present folds back upon and reorients it. Just as the incarnate self is perceived by others, it perceives them. And just as language is carried by my relationship to the world, the past, and others, it also helps carry them. Therefore, truth is formed in the lived present where all these chiasms take place. Merleau-Ponty says as much here as well.

> Our present expressive operations, instead of driving the preceding ones away—simply succeeding and annulling them—salvage, preserve, and (insofar as they contain some truth) take them up again; and the same phenomenon is produced in respect to others' expressive operations, whether they be past or contemporary. Our present keeps the promises of our past; we keep others' promises. (*Signs* 95)

> This is possible only through the same "intentional transgression" which gives us others; and like it the phenomenon of truth, which is theoretically impossible, is known only through the praxis which *creates* it. (*Signs* 95–96)

> To say there is a truth is to say that when my renewal meets the old or alien project, and successful expression frees what has always been held captive in being, an inner communication is established in the density of personal and interpersonal time through which our present becomes the truth of all the other knowing events. (*Signs* 96)

> At this moment something has been founded in signification; an experience has been transformed into its meaning, has become truth. Truth is another name for sedimentation, which is itself the presence of all presents in our own. (*Signs* 96)

This is not the modernist philosophy of presence so derided by Derrida and other postmodernists, since this is not the full presence of a meaning to a consciousness fully present to itself. Nor is it a postmodernist philosophy with no positive terms, a philosophy whose words are constantly deferring to other words. It is a philosophy in which the present opens out upon the temporal past and the spatial horizon—a temporal past and a spatial beyond with which it remains in contact, a contact which is *Ineinander* or chiasm, which can only be grasped in the act itself, and which when grasped is the very expression of truth.

"Thus," Merleau-Ponty concludes, "the proper function of a phenomenological philosophy seems to us to be to establish itself definitively in the order of instructive spontaneity" (*Signs* 97). This is an existential phenomenology that begins with the incarnate subject's lived act, the act that opens (*ek-stace*) the subject out on to a world and a temporality that runs beyond the subject but that includes the subject and others. It is therefore a world and temporality with which the subject prereflectively remains in contact. Where the active incarnate subject chiasmatically meets the world, the past, and others, there meaning and truth are formed. Hence meaning and truth are primarily and originally formed in the lived act, in an act that cannot be grasped or constructed from the outside but that must be lived from within, and that must be lived anew with each changing moment and event. But we should here give the last word to Merleau-Ponty.

> Now it is at the heart of my present that I find the meaning of those presents which preceded it, and that I find the means of understanding others' presence at the same world; and it is in the actual practice of speaking that I learn to understand. There is finality only in the sense in which Heidegger defined it when he said approximately that finality is the trembling of a unity exposed to contingency and tirelessly recreating itself. (*Signs* 97)

To summarize, we saw that Merleau-Ponty uncovers an inconsistency in Husserl's works, for the early Husserl develops an ideal essence of language that is used to make sense out of actual languages, while the later Husserl claims that the actual use of language is what enabled human beings to develop ideal thoughts or essences. This inconsistency can in part be accounted for by the conflicting points of view that are often taken with respect to language, the subjective view versus the objective view. Even Saussure, whom Merleau-Ponty often regards favorably, falls into this contradictory characterization of language, for he views language either synchronically (subjectively) or diachronically (objectively).

Merleau-Ponty claims that these views must be integrated rather than simply juxtaposed. It is this integration that he has sought here, and it is accomplished by the *Ineinander* (reversibility) phenomenon, the flowing into one another of subject and object, of self and other, of present and past, that occurs in the embodied subject's encounter with the world, others, and past. Language must likewise be understood as an *Ineinander* phenomenon. Language must be understood neither synchronically nor diachronically but as a system in the making, for the lived act of speech must constantly adjust the linguistic system to current events, just as the previous and present linguistic systems continually reorient each other. This gives rise to a new way of conceiving language, language that displays a concrete, incarnate logic.

As Merleau-Ponty claims in *Themes from the Lectures,* he claims here as well that language does say something, yet it does so, not as a collection of isolated words that refer singly to their own meaning, but as a whole system. However, this still does not mean that there is some sort of simple correspondence between the system of signs and its significations. Signs and significations must be understood as being in a relationship of reversibility. Speech and meaning fold in upon one another. Speech sublimates the body's lived perceptual encounter with the world by using the linguistic means available to help articulate the speechless intention, yet the linguistic means of expression plays a role in forming the meaning expressed. In addition, just as the means of expression fold back upon the body's perceptual intentions, they also aim out toward a field of already composed intentions which fold back upon and arouse them. Just as the body aims at the world that folds back upon it, the lived act of speech aims at a field of significations that folds back upon it, that folds back upon its means of expression helping to complete it. And just as the perceptual field is a gestalt structure of differential yet relational meanings, so the significative field is a gestalt structure of differential yet relational meanings. Just as perceptual meaning is stable yet indirect and even allusive, so also is linguistic meaning.

Finally, Merleau-Ponty's analysis of the relationship between language and experience leads him to reevaluate the relationship between philosophy and phenomenology. He finds yet another contradiction in Husserl, for Husserl at once claims both that phenomenology is merely a preparation for the abstract essences of philosophy and yet that the phenomenological descriptions of the life-world somehow remain in these abstract thoughts. For Merleau-Ponty phenomenology must start with the prereflective, lived activity of the incarnate subject, with the actual mode of presence of objects to the experience of the incarnate subject. Abstract thought, then, is a sublimation of this concrete encounter. The concrete is not a manifestation of an eidetic ideal. Moreover, the phenomenology of language makes clear that language helps form thought, that there is no philosophical thought outside of language. Significations and language exist in a relationship of reversibility to one another. This relationship is called *Ineinander* in the lecture notes and chiasm in the posthumous *The Visible and the Invisible*. It becomes the heart of Merleau-Ponty's incarnate existential phenomenology.

"Indirect Language and the Voices of Silence"

"Indirect Language and the Voices of Silence" was first published in 1952 but republished by Merleau-Ponty in *Signes* in 1960. The fact that he republishes it without alteration is proof enough that he still fully accepts its content. The original 1952 essay is a significantly rewritten version of the unpublished *The Prose of the World,* which, as Lefort claims, would not have been published in its original form. For it is in this manuscript that Merleau-Ponty first hits upon the idea of an indirect ontology, undoubtedly influenced by the indirect language that he finds in Saussure. Yet for Merleau-Ponty this by no means indicates that language creates ontology. As we have seen throughout, and as we will see in this essay, it is an indirect ontology that gives rise to an indirect language. We may say then that, in the order of discovery, Merleau-Ponty's insights into language lead to the thesis of an indirect ontology, but that in the order of ontology, the world and mute bodily perception precede linguistic expression.

Merleau-Ponty immediately opens this essay with a brief summary of Saussure's theory of language, which can be restated as follows. Language is a gestalt or dialectical whole. It is a system of differences. The words of this linguistic system take on a meaning only because of their place in the whole. Phonemes, even more so, form a system of differences. Moreover, a child may grasp the style of the whole language in one of its parts, even in the rhythm of a word's phonemic opposition. Or, as Merleau-Ponty summarily put it, "[A]s far as language is concerned, it is the lateral relation of one sign to another which makes each of them seem significant, that meaning appears at the intersection of . . . words." He proceeds to draw here a conclusion that he arrived at in both *Phenomenology of Perception* and *Themes from the Lectures*. "This characteristic prevents us from forming the usual conception of the distinction and the union between language and its meaning" (*Signs* 42). Language and meaning are now to be seen not as distinct but as intimately interwoven. Moreover, this blending of words and meaning also prevents language from being based on a system of already formed positive thoughts. There is no pregiven thought that exists prior to language that language simply translates. All of this means, as we will observe, that language is indirect, allusive, and even silent (*Signs* 43).

As we have just seen in the lecture notes and in "On the Phenomenology of Language," Merleau-Ponty conceives of language as being one manifestation of the reversibility phenomenon found in human experience. We have seen that where the active incarnate subject and the world meet, there meaning is formed. The activity and passivity of the body subject flow or cross into one another to the point where it is impossible to know where one begins and the other ends. This means that we cannot grasp the meaning of this experience reflectively or by reconstructing it from the outside. The only way to grasp this experience is by living it. Merleau-Ponty says much the same thing here about language. Just as words actively refer to meanings, these meanings fold back upon their means of expression to help articulate them. The only way that we can grasp this creation of meaning in language is by performing it ourselves. Furthermore, if this way of characterizing the act of linguistic expression is true, then it is also similar to the act of painting. For the painter, like the writer, "addresses himself to an unformulated power of deciphering within us that we control only after we have blindly used it" (*Signs* 45).

> Matisse looked at the still open whole of his work in progress and brought his brush toward the line which called for it in order that the painting might finally be that which it was in the process of becoming. (*Signs* 45–46)

> [In the same way the act of expressive speech] gropes around a significative intention which is not guided by any text, and which is precisely in the process of writing the text. (*Signs* 46)

Thus here again we find Merleau-Ponty focusing on the spontaneous creation of meaning, on the "unformulated power of deciphering within us" that can only be grasped in use, that can only be understood in actual performance—that cannot be intellectually or empirically constructed from the outside looking in.

In an obviously related point, Merleau-Ponty claims the classical (linear) perspective in painting (which depicts spatial recession by means of parallel lines and planes converging on a distant vanishing point) is only one option and not *the* form of representing space or the perceived world. The Cartesian coordinate system is an abstract rational construction of perceived space. It is not perceived space itself, which bends around and engulfs the subject, and within which objects are not perceived with a definite size relative to one another nor within a definite place in a rational grid. Perceived objects compete for attention, and when one wins the others slip into a horizontal background that helps articulate it.

But, Merleau-Ponty says, this rejection of an objective perspective does not mean that we pass into the subjective—as Malraux and others would have it. Merleau-Ponty has developed a philosophy which is not a philosophy of the subject, but a philosophy of chiasm, of *Ineinander,* of flowing into one another of subject and object, of self and other, of language and meaning. We have seen that human meaning is formed where the active incarnate subject encounters a contingent world. This incarnate perceptual meaning is formed as a gestalt, as a *lived structure* to which both the human body and the world contribute. This lived framework can be understood as a certain style, as a certain "coherent deformation" of the commonly perceived world. It is this style that the painter brings to perception and painting. It is a style formed only in interaction with the world, only through engagement with it, and not in an isolated subject cut off from the world.

The painter's style, then, cannot be cut off from the painter's perceptual contact with the world. And Merleau-Ponty points out that even Malraux admits this, for he admits that "perception already stylizes." (The actual phrase is Merleau-Ponty's.) Or, as Merleau-Ponty goes on to further express it: "For the painter, style is the system of equivalences that he makes . . . for the work which manifests the world he sees. It is the . . . 'coherent deformation' by which he concentrates the still scattered meaning of his perception and makes it exist expressly" (*Signs* 54–55). According to Merleau-Ponty, then, the painter (and the poet or writer) always says something about the world. A painting "is a new set of equivalences which demand precisely this particular upheaval, and it is in the name of a truer relation between things that their ordinary ties are broken" (*Signs* 56).

> It is always only a question of advancing the line at the already opened furrow and of recapturing and generalizing an accent which has already appeared in the corner of a previous painting or in some instant of his experience, without the painter himself ever being able to say (since the destination has no meaning) what comes from him and what comes from the things, what the new work adds to the old ones, or what it has taken from the others and what is its own. (*Signs* 58–59)

Here again we see Merleau-Ponty returning to the chiasm phenomenon, in this case the flowing into one another of painter and world, of the past and present, and of the incarnate self and the other. We have already seen that just as the past orients the present, the present simultaneously reorients the past. The moments of human time existentially remain open to one another. In the same way my empathic relationship to the other can reverse my constitutive intentions toward the other, can snap up my behavior and constitute me. My active and passive relationships toward the other partially blend. Within these lived experiences, then, I can take up the past and the gestures of the other and, as I partially blend with them, can carry them forward.

Merleau-Ponty goes on to say that "this triple resumption" of the world, the past, and others "makes a sort of provisory eternity of the operations of expression," that is, makes possible the linking of human expressions, and therefore makes possible a human history (*Signs* 59). Yet what links individual acts (my own and mine with those of others, past and present) to provide a history is not some Hegelian Spirit or Reason. Merleau-Ponty claims that we will only understand what links these acts "when the theory of perception makes the painter dwell once more in the visible world and once more lays bare the body as spontaneous expression" (*Signs* 65). Merleau-Ponty is able to make this claim because he believes we are able to witness the same style in an artist's miniatures and full-sized works, and because he believes we can understand this only if we grasp in the body a "general motor power of formation capable of the transpositions which constitute the constancy of style" (*Signs* 65). The human body must be understood as a general motor power which utilizes various structures, various habitual ways of confronting and organizing the world in a way that allows the transposition of one into another (*Signs* 67). And indeed, if this is the case, "the movement of the artist tracing his arabesque in infinite matter amplifies, but also prolongs, the simple marvel of oriented locomotion or grasping movements" (*Signs* 67). Painting, then, is one example of the body's power of oriented movement; it prolongs it and expresses it at a higher level. Yet Merleau-Ponty makes an even broader claim, one that we have seen indicated above. "All perception, all action which presupposes it, and in short every human use of the body is already primordial expression" (*Signs* 67). Not only does the artist make use of the body's power of oriented movement, but all actions *are* already this *oriented* movement, are already a primordial expression of meaning. Moreover, since all perception involves bodily movement, a bodily movement that is oriented, i.e., that organizes perception in a meaningful way, all perception is already a form of expression. We now have the means of grasping how actions can be historically linked to one another. It is because all human gestures create a meaning and refer beyond themselves that all human gestures are comparable—at least in a general sense (*Signs* 68). It is because all human bodily actions are meaningfully oriented toward the world that they may be used to understand one another, that one may slip into another.

> Despite the diversity of its parts . . . , the body is capable of gathering itself into a gesture which for a time dominates their dispersion and puts its stamp upon everything it does. In the same way, we may speak of a unity of human style which transcends spatial and temporal distances to bring the gestures of all painters together in one single cumulative history—a single act. The enveloping movement which the unity of culture extends beyond the limits of the individual life is of the same type as that which unites all the moments of the individual life itself. (*Signs* 68–69)

Thus, it is because all actions of the body are an oriented meaningful movement that they are comparable and can slip into one another. This linking occurs within the individual and, because human beings have similar bodies, between individuals. The unity of culture and the unity of history are made possible, then, by the lived unity of the body. Yet, again, this unity of culture is not to be compared with some type of Hegelian Spirit. Just as the body maintains itself and the unity of its acts only by being in the world, the history of painting or the unity of culture is maintained only by the actual efforts to take up the past and express something new. There is no history, at least no meaningful history, apart from the human actions that meaningfully take up past events and carry them into the future.

Yet even though painting and language are similar as acts of expression, and even though Merleau-Ponty's comments thus far can be applied to both, he proceeds now to distinguish them.

> Thus, when we compare language to mute forms of expression such as gestures or paintings, we must point out that unlike these forms language is not content to sketch out directions, vectors, a "coherent deformation," or a tacit meaning on the surface of the world, exhausting itself as animal "intelligence" does in kaleidoscopically producing a new landscape of action. Language is not just the replacement of one meaning by another, but the substitution of equivalent meanings. The new structure is given as already present in the old, the latter subsists in it, and the past is now understood. (*Signs* 81)

Once again Merleau-Ponty's idea of the reversibility phenomenon enlightens here. For if the past and the present fold in upon one another, if the past influences the present at the same time the present reorients the past, and if language participates in this phenomenon, then language must also be characterized as a chiasm phenomenon, as taking up a past that it is influenced by, but as also reorienting this past with a new structure to allow it to be more fully understood. Language involves a higher level of sublimation, a higher level of integration or reorientation that allows for a more complete understanding of the original experience that gives rise to it. Yet this understanding, this meaning never occurs without the language which bears it.

> What we *mean* is not before us, outside all speech, as sheer signification. It is only the excess of what we live over what has already been said. With our apparatus of expression we set ourselves up in a situation the apparatus is sensitive to, we confront it with the situation, and our statements are only the final balance of these exchanges. Political thought itself is of this order. It is always the elucidation of a historical perception in which all our understandings, all our experiences, and all our values simultaneously come into play—and of which our theses are only the schematic formulation. (*Signs* 83)

This means that abstract significations are never pure, that is, never occur outside of all speech, as modernists have claimed, yet this also means that language does not get its meaning simply from itself, as many postmodernists currently claim. It gets its meaning by our full participation in the life-world, with all its chiasms and reversals. Because of the importance that postmodernist and deconstructionist philosophies have taken on today with their seeming abandonment of perception and the life-world for an omnicreative language, Merleau-Ponty's comments here take on special significance and act, perhaps, as a corrective to these exaggerated linguistic views.

> Yet try as each word may (as Saussure explains) to extract its meaning from all the others, the fact remains that at the moment it occurs the task of expressing is no longer differentiated and referred to other words—it is accomplished, and we understand something. Saussure may show that each act of expression becomes significant only as in modulation of a general system of expression and only insofar as it is differentiated from other linguistic gestures. The marvel is that before Saussure we did not know anything about this, and we forget it again each time we speak . . . This proves that each partial act of expression . . . is not limited to expending an expressive power accumulated in the language, but recreates both the power and the language by making us verify . . . the power that speaking subjects have of going beyond signs toward their meaning. Signs do not simply evoke other signs for us and so on without

> end, and language is not like a prison we are locked into or a guide we must follow blindly; for what these linguistic gestures mean . . . finally appears at the intersection of all of them. (*Signs* 81)

For Merleau-Ponty, contra the postmodernists, language is not just about itself; words do not just constantly defer to other words. They do this but they also say something. They refer to a meaning. They refer to a meaning that slips beyond the means of expression but that does not exist without them. Meaning does not exist without language, yet it folds back upon its means of expression to help pull them together and articulate them. Moreover, linguistic gestures themselves are a prolongation of the body's perceptual encounter with the world.

To summarize, we have seen in "Indirect Language and the Voices of Silence" that Merleau-Ponty once again agrees with Saussure's characterization of language as a diacritical system of differences, as words and phonemes referring laterally to one another, and that language nevertheless also does refer beyond itself to a meaning. Unlike the traditional/modernist view of language, Merleau-Ponty refuses to separate sign and signification. Sound and meaning, word and thought are interwoven. Language refers beyond itself to a meaning, but this meaning does not exist without its means of expression, and, moreover, this meaning folds back upon its means of expression to help articulate them. Thus the relationship between sign and signification as we have seen it expressed here is one more manifestation of the reversibility phenomenon that we have seen expressed in the posthumous text, in the lecture notes, and in "On the Phenomenology of Language."

We have also seen Merleau-Ponty further explore the reversibility phenomenon by comparing linguistic expression and the act of painting. In the act of painting, where the incarnate self comes into lived and reversible contact with the world, others, and the past, a meaning and a style are formed. They are formed concretely in the lived act and cannot be constructed either intellectually or empirically. The act of perception is already a "going beyond," for the human body prereflectively gathers scattered elements of perception and relates them meaningfully. The painter's style then is always formed in contact with the world and is always about the world. Even when the painter takes up previous expressions, advances a line or a mode of expression, and says something new, this something new is still about the world, is a "coherent deformation" of it. This past that orients the present is taken up in the present act and confirmed, prolonged, and subsequently reoriented. A history is therefore formed, and this history is made possible by the human body. For it is the body that links acts within me and links those within me with those of others. The body is able to link acts within me because it is a "general motor power . . . capable of transposition." The body is able to link my acts with those of others because "every human use of the body is already primordial expression." Already the act of perception is a primordial expression, a "going beyond" the simply given, a prereflective gathering of elements into a meaningful organization. All human gestures refer beyond themselves to create a meaning. Therefore all human gestures are comparable at least in this general sense. This is what allows us to link acts historically. That is to say, it is because all human bodily actions are meaningfully oriented toward the world that they may be used to understand one another, that they may slip into one another. The unity of culture and history are made possible by the unity of the body.

Painting and writing are similar, Merleau-Ponty has said here, for they are both expressive bodily gestures, but they are also different. Painting "sketch[es] out directions, vectors, a 'coherent deformation' . . . on the surface of the world." Language is more of a sublimation, a replacing of a meaning at a higher level of generalization that folds back upon its origins to help enlighten and reorient them. Language is able to continually do this, is able to continually create new systems of understanding, but is always rooted in the body's lived sensuous encounter with the world. Language thus exists in a relationship of nonreciprocal reversibility with the perceptual world upon which it rests.

Merleau-Ponty's view of language as we have seen it expressed here and throughout his later works is certainly not modernist, in the philosophical sense, nor is it postmodernist in the sense this word has taken since his death in 1961, especially in the sense of the deconstructionist philosophy of Derrida. We have seen that *Phenomenology of Perception* already argues explicitly against the modern view of language, in both its rationalist and empiricist forms. The rationalist regards the word as an empty vehicle for thought already formed, while the empiricist interprets the word as a sound blindly associated with a perceived object or its representation. We have seen that Merleau-Ponty attempts to defeat both rationalism and empiricism by claiming that the word itself has a meaning. Against the rationalist he argues that there is no pure *thought* apart from language. And against the empiricist he argues that words have a meaning for the speaking subject, that they cannot be accounted for simply as an objective, third-person process. Later, in *The Visible and the Invisible,* in *Themes from the Lectures,* in "On the Phenomenology of Language," and here in "Indirect Language and the Voices of Silence," we have seen Merleau-Ponty more generally argue against philosophical modernism and its idea that thought is separate from expression, for he has claimed that thought and expression are inextricably bound together. Signification and sign exist in a relationship of nonreciprocal reversibility, in a relationship of chiasm. Moreover, we have seen Merleau-Ponty at least implicitly argue against what has since come to be called "postmodernism," against its idea that expression can be separated from the embodied subject, from its perceptual encounter with the world.

We have seen that Merleau-Ponty's philosophy begins with the lived body thrown into the world. Consciousness is the body's openness unto and directedness toward the world. Where the active body and the forces and patterns of the world meet, there meaning is formed. Moreover, since perception is already a "going beyond," since it meaningfully relates parts of the perceptual field to one another, perception is already expression. This bodily expression is prolonged in another bodily expression, one that is called speech. Linguistic gestures sublimate perceptual gestures, and my perceptual and linguistic gestures slip into those of other human subjects and those of the past, a past we all remain in contact with, as it orients us and we reorient it.

Merleau-Ponty's philosophy, as it has just been characterized, is not a "modern" philosophy. It does not embrace the Cartesian idea of one rational world grasped by one geometrically rational system. Merleau-Ponty's philosophy does not embrace the idea of independent ontological substances but reveals overlapping ontological regions by means of lived-through bodily perception. In fact, perception itself is nothing but a bit of matter folding over on itself and becoming aware of itself. Perception is an intentionality that occurs within Being and that reveals the multifariousness of Being through its own encounter with the variety of beings.

Merleau-Ponty's philosophy has no exact precedent in the history of philosophy. It perhaps has its closest affinity with the American pragmatists, particularly with the works of John Dewey and George Herbert Mead.[4] But his philosophy is not to be associated with Derrida's philosophy of deconstruction or with its American cousin, Richard Rorty's pragmatism. Rorty wants to get beyond the "raw feels" of consciousness[5] and Derrida separates language from the lived embodied perceptual encounter with the world. Language, according to Derrida, has no transcendental referent; signifiers refer to other signifiers, and so on, without end. For Merleau-Ponty language refers beyond itself to a really existing world, a world that humans encounter bodily at every turn. Moreover, language also refers to a field of meanings that is a sublimation of this body/world encounter. Merleau-Ponty's view is therefore less alienated from the body and its perceptual encounter with the world. His philosophy does not claim that language alone creates all meaning, but more reasonably places language in a chiasmatic relationship with the body and lived world.

Merleau-Ponty's philosophy is not a philosophy of the Cartesian or Sartrean ego, for there is no intersubjectivity in these positions. Nor is his philosophy a philosophy of the social as "social fact," for there is no person or subject in this position. Merleau-Ponty's philosophy is a philosophy of the embodied subject that *is* a carnal relationship to the world. Consciousness is *ek-stace,* is *at* the object in the world through the human body. Prereflective embodied consciousness has an anonymous dimension. The individuated self blends into an anonymous bodily self and an anonymous visibility. Embodied consciousness is a relationship to the world that includes it and others. There is a chiasm between self and other, self and world. There is a chiasm between the self and the social. Yet for Merleau-Ponty this social is not a fact observed or constructed from the outside. The social is a set of institutions, and these institutions are to be understood as efficacious systems of symbols that are inserted into the individual (*Signs* 115).

> Living language is precisely that togetherness of thinking and thing which causes the difficulty. In the act of speaking, the subject, in his tone and his style, bears witness to his autonomy, since nothing is more proper to him, and yet at the same moment, and without contradiction, he is turned toward the linguistic community and is dependent on his language. The will to speak is one and the same as the will to be understood. The presence of the individual in the institution and of the institution in the individual is evident in the case of linguistic change. (*IPP* 54–55)

This chiasm between self and language is the means by which the social is expressed in the individual and the individual is expressed in the social. The individual is not collapsed into social or into linguistic relationships, nor are these relationships created by themselves or by isolated individuals. The self and the social, the self and language must be seen to form a system, must be seen in a chiasmatic relationship to one another.

> The reciprocal relations between the will to express and the means of expression correspond to those between the productive forces and the forms of production, and, more generally, between historical forces and institutions. Just as language is a system of signs which have meaning only in relation to one another . . . so each institution is a symbolic system that the subject takes over and incorporates as a style of functioning, as a global configuration, without having any need to conceive it at all. When

> equilibrium is destroyed, the reorganizations which take place comprise, like those of language, an internal logic even though it may not be clearly thought out by anyone. They are polarized by the fact that, as participants in a system of symbols, we exist in the eyes of one another, with one another in such a way that changes in language are due to our will to speak and be understood. (*IPP* 55–56)

For Merleau-Ponty the social must be understood as embodied subjects opening out upon and partially blending with a shared field, a field of perceptual events and symbolic institutions. As each individual takes up these events and institutions and seeks recognition within their context, a social history is formed.

Merleau-Ponty's later philosophy has found a remarkable balance between self and others, self and world, present and past, sign and signification, and so on. It is a philosophy that does not reduce one element of experience to any of the others but that finds all of them flowing in upon one another. It is a philosophy of the dialectical whole. Yet this dialectical philosophy does not create the confusion of everything connected equally to everything else. It finds patterns of sense, gestalts of unfolding meaning. It is a philosophy whose explanatory power is superior precisely because it does find structures and patterns within experience without reducing all of experience to only one of its elements, whether that element be nature in itself, consciousness for itself, or a self-generating language.

Notes

Preface

1. Maurice Merleau-Ponty, *The Visible and the Invisible: Followed by Working Notes,* edited by Claude Lefort and translated by Alphonso Lingis (Evanston: Northwestern University Press, 1968). Originally published as *Le Visible et l'invisible: suivi de notes de travail,* edited by Claude Lefort (Paris: Gallimard, 1964).

2. Gary Madison, "Did Merleau-Ponty Have a Theory of Perception?" in *Merleau-Ponty, Hermeneutics and Postmodernism,* edited by T. Busch and T. Gallagher (Albany: State University of New York Press, 1992), 83–106.

3. Douglas Low, "The Continuity Between Merleau-Ponty's Early and Late Philosophy of Language," *Journal of Philosophical Research* 17 (1992): 287–311, especially 304 ff.

4. Ibid. See also Douglas Low, "Merleau-Ponty's Intertwined Notions of Subjectivity and Intersubjectivity," *International Studies in Philosophy* 24, no. 3 (1992): 45–64, especially 56.

5. I have also attempted to do this elsewhere. See Douglas Low, "Merleau-Ponty's Concept of Reason," *Journal of Philosophical Research* 19 (1994): 109–25; and "Merleau-Ponty and the Foundations of Multiculturalism," *Journal of Philosophical Research* 21 (1996): 377–90.

6. James Schmidt, *Maurice Merleau-Ponty: Between Phenomenology and Structuralism* (New York: St. Martin's Press, 1985), 9, where multiple interpretations are discussed.

Introduction

The epigraph is an introductory note by Martial Gueroult preceding his "Un inédit de Merleau-Ponty," *Revue de métaphysique et de morale,* no. 4 (1962): 401–9. This text and Gueroult's comments are translated by Arleen Dallery under the title "An Unpublished Test by Merleau-Ponty: A Prospectus of His Work" and reprinted in Merleau-Ponty's *The Primacy of Perception,* edited by James Edie (Evanston: Northwestern University Press, 1964), 3–11. See also Merleau-Ponty's *The Prose of the World,* edited by Claude Lefort and translated by John O'Neill (Evanston: Northwestern University Press, 1973), xiii–xiv.

There is reason to believe that the study *L'Origine de la vérite* mentioned by Gueroult in the epigraph was eventually retitled as *Le Visible et l'invisible.* See Merleau-Ponty, *The Visible and the Invisible,* xxxiv.

1. See preface note 1 above.

2. *VI* xxxvi.

3. *VI* xxxvi.

4. *VI* 165–75.

5. Merleau-Ponty, *Themes from the Lectures at the Collège de France, 1952–1960,* translated by John O'Neill (Evanston: Northwestern University Press, 1970).

6. Merleau-Ponty, *The Prose of the World.*

7. Lefort's *PW* preface xvii, where he states: "At the Collège de France, [Merleau-Ponty] chose as the subject of his first two courses, in 1953–54, 'The Sensible World and Expression' and 'The Literary Use of Language' "; and a little further on: "In the following year, he again considers 'The Problem of Speech.' " These lectures make up part of the series presented in *Themes from the Lectures.*

8. Lefort's *PW* preface xx.

9. "L'Oeil et l'esprit" first appeared in *Art de France* 1, no. 1 (January 1961). "Eye and Mind" is translated by Carleton Dallery and appears in *The Primacy of Perception,* edited by James Edie (Evanston: Northwestern University Press, 1964).

10. Merleau-Ponty, *Signs,* translated by Richard McCleary (Evanston: Northwestern University Press, 1964).

11. See *VI* 165, where Merleau-Ponty writes: "Draw up the picture of wild Being, prolonging my article on Husserl." Lefort cites the following as the article on Husserl referred to by Merleau-Ponty: "The Philosopher and His Shadow," in *Edmund Husserl, 1859–1959 Recueil commemoratif* (The Hague, 1959); republished in *Signes* (Paris: Gallimard, 1960). This article assisted my interpretation of this chapter.

12. See also Gail Stenstad, "Merleau-Ponty's Logos: The Sens-ing of the Flesh," *Philosophy Today* 37 (Spring 1993): 52–61; and *VI* 149–55.

Chapter 1

1. *Merleau-Ponty in Contemporary Perspective,* edited by Patrick Burke and Jan Van der Veken (Boston: Kluwer Academic Publishers, 1993). Papers were presented in November 1991 at an international symposium on Merleau-Ponty, sponsored by the Institute of Philosophy and Husserl Archives at the Catholic University of Louvain.

2. Merleau-Ponty, *Phenomenology of Perception* (London: Routledge and Kegan Paul, 1962), 6th printing (1974), with corrected translation, xiii.

3. Merleau-Ponty, *Phenomenology of Perception,* 70.

4. M. C. Dillon, *Semiological Reductionism: A Critique of the Deconstructionist Movement in Postmodern Thought* (Albany: State University of New York Press, 1995), provides an excellent critique of deconstruction from the viewpoint of Merleau-Ponty's thought. See also Dillon, "Merleau-Ponty and Postmodernity,"

in *Merleau-Ponty Vivant,* edited by M. C. Dillon (Albany: State University of New York Press, 1991), xxvi–xxix. See also Jacques Taminiaux, "Phenomenology in Merleau-Ponty's Late Work," in *Life-World and Consciousness,* edited by L. E. Embree (Evanston: Northwestern University Press, 1972), 307–22. The pertinent passages from Jacques Derrida's works can be found in *Speech and Phenomena,* translated by D. Allison (Evanston: Northwestern University Press, 1973), 104, 139 ff., and 152 ff.; and in "Structure, Sign and Play in the Discourse of Human Sciences" in *The Structuralist Controversy,* edited by R. Mackey and E. Danto (Baltimore: Johns Hopkins University Press, 1972), 272.

5. Merleau-Ponty, *Phenomenology of Perception,* xiv, where he argues that the reduction is never complete.

Chapter 2

1. Edmund Husserl, *Meditations Cartesiennes* (Paris, 1947), 33. English translation, *Cartesian Meditations,* by Dorian Cairns (The Hague: Martinus Nijhoff, 1960), 38–39.

Chapter 3

1. Marjorie Grene, "Merleau-Ponty and the Renewal of Ontology," *Review of Metaphysics* 29, no. 4 (June 1976): 605–25. Grene discusses Merleau-Ponty's later notion of lateral evolution and attempts to reconcile it with his earlier idea of hierarchical development, which was expressed in *The Structure of Behavior,* translated by A. Fisher (Boston: Beacon Press, 1963).

2. M. C. Dillon, *Merleau-Ponty's Ontology* (Evanston: Northwestern University Press, 1997), 94 ff., 208 ff.

Chapter 4

1. Jean-Paul Sartre, *Situations,* translated by Benita Eisler (New York: George Braziller, 1965), 321. Originally published as *Situations IV* (Paris: Gallimard, 1964).

2. For a brief reference to how this terminology is used, see "Modern Art," in *The New Encyclopaedia Britannica,* 15th ed., Micropaedia, vol. 8 (Chicago: Encyclopaedia Britannica, 1991), 214.

Chapter 5

1. M. C. Dillon, "Apriority in Kant and Merleau-Ponty," *Kant-Studies* 17 (1987): 403–23, offers an analysis of the similarity and difference between Kant

and Merleau-Ponty; see particularly 417 and 419 ff. Here is a concluding remark: "Kant grounds his apriori in the necessity/immutability of the structures of mind which provides the foundation for the laws of temporal synthesis conceived as formal principles supervenient upon the sensuous matter of experience. Merleau-Ponty seeks as well for principles of synthesis—concepts—capable of unifying experience, but for Merleau-Ponty, the synthetic principles are grounded in the phenomenal world rather than in the mind, and they are conceived as subject to modification as the world unfolds" (420).

2. Edmund Husserl, *Die Krisis der europäischen Wissenschaften und die transzendentale Phanomenologie,* edited by Walter Biemel, *Husserlian VI* (The Hague: Martinus Nijhoff, 1962), 365–86. English translation, *The Crisis of European Sciences and Transcendental Phenomenology,* by David Carr (Evanston: Northwestern University Press, 1970).

3. Unpublished text by Edmund Husserl.

4. Sandra Rosenthal and Patrick Bourgeois, *Mead and Merleau-Ponty: Toward Common Vision* (Albany: State University of New York Press, 1991).

5. Richard Rorty, *Philosophy and the Mirror of Nature* (Princeton: Princeton University Press, 1979), especially 70 ff.

Bibliography

Works by Merleau-Ponty

Adventures of the Dialectic. Translated by Joseph Bien. Evanston: Northwestern University Press, 1973; London: Heineman, 1974. Originally published as *Les Aventures de la dialectique.* Paris: Gallimard, 1955.

Consciousness and the Acquisition of Language. Translated by Hugh J. Silverman. Evanston: Northwestern University Press, 1973. Originally published as "La Conscience et l'acquisition du language." *Bulletin de psychologie* 18, no. 236 (1964): 3–6.

"The Experience of Others." Translated by Fred Evans and Hugh J. Silverman. *Review of Existential Psychology and Psychiatry* 18 (1982–83). Originally published as "L'Expérience d'autrui." *Bulletin du groupe d'études de psychologie de l'Université de Paris* (1951–52). Paris: Centre de Documentation Universitaire.

Humanism and Terror: An Essay on the Communist Problem. Translated by John O'Neill. Boston: Beacon Press, 1969. Originally published as *Humanisme et terreur, essai sur le probleme communiste.* Paris: Gallimard, 1947.

In Praise of Philosophy. Translated by John Wild and James M. Edie. Evanston: Northwestern University Press, 1963. Originally published as *Eloge de la philosophie et autres essais.* Paris: Gallimard, 1960.

Phenomenology of Perception. Translated by Colin Smith. New York: Humanities Press, 1962; London: Routledge and Kegan Paul, 1962. Sixth printing 1974, which includes translation corrections. Originally published as *Phénoménologie de la perception.* Paris: Gallimard, 1945.

"Philosophy and Non-Philosophy since Hegel." Translated by Hugh J. Silverman. In *Philosophy and Non-Philosophy since Merleau-Ponty.* London: Routledge, 1988. Originally "Philosophie et non-philosophie depuis Hegel," a summary of Merleau-Ponty's 1961 course at the Collège de France. It was prepared for presentation by Claude Lefort and appeared in *Textures,* nos. 8–9 and 10–11 (1974). See Lefort's "Presenting Merleau-Ponty" in *Telos,* no. 29 (Fall 1976): 39–42, followed by Silverman's first translation of "Philosophie et non-philosophie depuis Hegel," 106–29.

The Primacy of Perception and Other Essays. Edited by James M. Edie. Evanston: Northwestern University Press, 1964. Title essay originally published as "Le Primat de la perception et ses conséquences philosophiques," 1946.

The Prose of the World. Translated by John O'Neill. Evanston: Northwestern University Press, 1973. Originally published as *La Prose du monde.* Edited by Claude Lefort. Paris: Gallimard, 1969. (Posthumous publication)

Sense and Nonsense. Translated by Herbert L. Dreyfus and Patricia Allen Dreyfus. Evanston: Northwestern University Press, 1964. Originally published as *Sens et non-sens.* Paris: Nagel, 1948.

Signs. Translated by Richard C. McCleary. Evanston: Northwestern University Press, 1964. Originally published as *Signes.* Paris: Gallimard, 1960.

The Structure of Behavior. Translated by Alden L. Fisher. Boston: Beacon Press, 1963; London: Methuen, 1965. Originally published as *La Structure du comportement.* Paris: Presses Universitaires de France, 1942.

Themes from the Lectures at the Collège de France, 1952–1960. Translated by John O'Neill. Evanston: Northwestern University Press, 1970. Originally published as *Résumés des cours, Collège de France, 1952–1960.* Paris: Gallimard, 1968.

The Visible and the Invisible: Followed by Working Notes. Translated by Alphonso Lingis. Evanston: Northwestern University Press, 1968. Originally published as *Le Visible et l'invisible: suivi de notes de travail.* Edited by Claude Lefort. Paris: Gallimard, 1964.

Other Sources

Bourgeois, Patrick. "The Integration of Merleau-Ponty's Philosophy." *Southwest Philosophical Studies* 5 (July 1989): 37–50.

Busch, Thomas, and Thomas Gallagher, eds. *Merleau-Ponty, Hermeneutics and Postmodernism.* Albany: State University of New York Press, 1992.

Derrida, Jacques. *Speech and Phenomena.* Evanston: Northwestern University Press, 1973.

———. "Structure, Sign and Play in the Discourse of Human Sciences." In *The Structuralist Controversy.* Edited by R. Mackey and E. Danto. Baltimore: Johns Hopkins University Press, 1972.

Descartes, René. *Meditations on First Philosophy.* Translated by L. Lafleur. New York: Macmillan, 1985.

Descombes, Vincent. *Modern French Philosophy.* Translated by L. Scott-Fox and J. M. Harding. Cambridge: Cambridge University Press, 1980.

Dillon, Martin C. "Merleau-Ponty and Postmodernity." In *Merleau-Ponty Vivant.* Edited by Martin C. Dillon. Albany: State University of New York Press, 1991. ix–xxxv.

———. "Merleau-Ponty and the Transcendence of Immanence: Overcoming the Ontology of Consciousness." *Man and World* 19 (1986): 395–410.

———. *Merleau-Ponty's Ontology.* Evanston: Northwestern University Press, 1997.

———. *Semiological Reductionism: A Critique of the Deconstructionist Movement in Postmodern Thought.* Albany: State University of New York Press, 1995.

Flynn, Bernard. "Textuality of the Flesh: Derrida and Merleau-Ponty." *Journal of British Society for Phenomenology* 15 (1987): 164–77.

Grene, Marjorie. "Merleau-Ponty and the Renewal of Ontology." *Review of Metaphysics* 29, no. 4 (June 1976): 605–25.

Heidegger, Martin. *Being and Time.* Translated by J. Macquarrie and E. Robinson. New York: Harper and Row, 1962. Originally published as *Sein und Zeit,* I. Halle, 1927.

Holland, Nancy. "Merleau-Ponty on Presence: A Derridian Reading." *Research on Phenomenology* 16 (1986): 111–20.

Hume, David. *An Inquiry Concerning Human Understanding.* Chicago: Open Court, 1927.

Husserl, Edmund. *Cartesian Meditations.* Translated by Dorian Cairns. The Hague: Martinus Nijhoff, 1960. Originally published as *Meditations Cartesiennes.* Paris, 1947.

———. *The Crisis of European Sciences and Transcendental Phenomenology.* Translated by David Carr. Northwestern University Press, 1970. Originally published as *Die Krisis der europäischen Wissenschaften und die transzendentale Phanomenologie.* Edited by Walter Biemel. *Husserlian VI.* The Hague: Martinus Nijhoff, 1962.

Low, Douglas. "The Continuity between Merleau-Ponty's Early and Late Philosophy of Language." *Journal of Philosophical Research* 17 (1992): 287–311.

———. *The Existential Dialectic of Marx and Merleau-Ponty.* New York: Peter Lang, 1987.

———. "Merleau-Ponty and the Foundations of Multiculturalism." *Journal of Philosophical Research* 21 (1996): 377–90.

———. "Merleau-Ponty's Concept of Reason." *Journal of Philosophical Research* 19 (1994): 109–25.

———. "Merleau-Ponty's Intertwined Notions of Subjectivity and Intersubjectivity." *International Studies in Philosophy* 24, no. 3 (1992): 45–64.

Madison, Gary Brent. *The Phenomenology of Merleau-Ponty: A Search for the Limits of Consciousness.* Athens: Ohio University Press, 1981.

Rorty, Richard. *Philosophy and the Mirror of Nature.* Princeton: Princeton University Press, 1979.

Rosenthal, Sandra, and Patrick Bourgeois. *Mead and Merleau-Ponty: Toward a Common Vision.* Albany: State University of New York Press, 1991.

Sartre, Jean-Paul. *Being and Nothingness.* New York: Washington Square Press, 1953. Originally published as *L'être et le néant.* Paris: Gallimard, 1943.

———. *Critique of Dialectical Reason.* Vol. 1. Translated by A. Sheridan-Smith. London: NLB, 1976. Vol. 2. Paris: Gallimard, 1985. Originally published as *Critique de raison dialectique, precede de question de method.* Paris: Gallimard, 1960.

———. *Situations.* Translated by Benita Eisler. New York: George Braziller, 1965. Originally published as *Situations IV.* Paris: Gallimard, 1964.

Schmidt, James. *Maurice Merleau-Ponty: Between Phenomenology and Structuralism.* New York: St. Martin's Press, 1985.

Stenstad, Gail. "Merleau-Ponty's Logos: The Sens-ing of the Flesh." 37 *Philosophy Today* (Spring 1993): 52–61.

Taminiaux, Jacques. "Phenomenology in Merleau-Ponty's Late Work." In *Life-World and Consciousness.* Edited by L. E. Embree. Evanston: Northwestern University Press, 1972.

Index

Aristotle, 24
art, 79, 104; and Being, 56–61, 67–68. *See also* painting
Art de France (periodical), 5
Augustine, Saint, 10

behavior: animal, 49, 81–82; lectures on, 48–49; way of behaving (*Gebaren*), 97–98
Being, 9, 37, 110; art and, 56, 61, 67–68; classical ontology and, 61; dehiscence and, 23, 28, 67; essence and, 16–17; in painting (inspiration and expiration of), 59, 64; language/speech and, 26; meaning of, 31; perception and, 15; relationship with, 28; as theme of philosophy, 9, 11
Bergson, Henri-Louis, 16, 23, 25, 41–42
body (human), the: bodily consciousness, *see* consciousness; bodily gestures, 23, 34, 75, 94–95, 105–6, 109, 110; body-world relationship, 12–13, 16, 21, 42–43, 54, 58, 84, 89, 97, (chiasm manifested in) 99; dehiscence of,18, 21, 32, 33–34; and experience, 30, 32; as "general motor power," 105, 108; and norms, 74; and phenomenon of incarnation, 97; symbolism in, 50, 55, 89; two aspects of, 25–26

Cartesian Meditations (Husserl), 37
Cartesian thought. *See* Descartes, René, and Cartesian thought
Cézanne, Paul, 56, 63–64
chiasm, 59, 88, 89, 99, 100, 102, 111; and the body, 18, 25, 34, 52, 55; and meaning of words, 33, 34, 35, 86, 107; philosophy of, 104
coincidence, 23, 25; language and, 26
Collège de France, 1, 3, 89, 99
consciousness, 17, 32, 38–39, 41, 97; perceptual/embodied, 42–43, 46, 52–54, 72, 110, 111; philosophy of, 80
constitution, concept of, 80, 90, 97
coordinate system. *See* Descartes, René, and Cartesian thought
Copernican view, 88, 89

Da Vinci, Leonardo, 65
Darwin, Charles, and Darwinian thought, 50, 51
deconstruction, 17–18, 24, 26, 27, 107, 110
dehiscence, 17–18, 21, 32, 33–34; and Being, 23, 28, 67
Derrida, Jacques, 17, 18, 26, 94, 100, 110
Descartes, René, and Cartesian thought, 16, 29, 43, 60–62, 110, 111; and consciousness, 32, 46, 53, 80; coordinate system of, 4, 44, 45, 63, 64, 103–4; and modernism, 45, 68; ontology of, 4, 39–40, 47, 56, 59; outmoded, 47; and reflection, 16; theory of vision, 59–62, 65, 66
Dewey, John, 110
Dillon, M. C., 55, 73
disclosure theory of truth, 15
Driesch, A. E., 51
dualism, 47

Eddington, Arthur Stanley, Sir, 48
eidetic reduction, eidetic ideal, 18, 91, 92, 93, 102
ek-stace, 17, 59, 81, 85, 111
Electra conflict, 82
empiricism, 77, 109

entelechy, 49
essences, 16–17, 18–20
evolution, 50, 51–52
existential phenomenology, 35, 36, 98, 100, 102
experience, 11–12, 14–15, 16, 20, 23–24, 25; the body and, 30, 32; "fabric of," 18; language/speech and, 27, 79–80, 86–87, 101; passivity in, 83–85. *See also* perception
expression: paradoxes of, 76; perceptual, 73, 74. *See also* language

Freud, Sigmund, 54

gestalts, perceptual, 33, 36, 52, 71–72, 101; visual (in painting), 65–66, 104
gestures, 23, 34, 75, 94–95, 105–6, 109, 110
gnosis, 74
Goldstein, Kurt, 79
"good error," 25–26
Gueroult, Martial, 1

Hegel, Georg Wilhelm Friedrich, and Hegelian thought, 80, 83, 90, 105, 106
Heidegger, Martin, 100
historicity, 85, 90
homosexuality, 55
humanism and nature, 40
Humboldt, Wilhelm von, 94
Husserl, Edmund, and Husserlian thought, 16, 18, 20, 37, 80; analysis of, 39, 42–44, 85–89, 99; on Being, 28, 37; inconsistency in, 96, 100, 101; and phenomenology of language, 91–93, 97

idealism, 13–14, 23, 42; phenomenology different from, 52; rejected, 48
ideality, 85, 87–88, 90
ideas, language and, 31–35, 71–72
imprinting, 81–82
inspiration, 59
institution, concept of, 80–83, 90
"interior life," 11
invisible, the, 53, 71, 72

Jakobson, Roman, 78

Kant, Immanuel, and Kantian thought, 16, 40, 41, 75, 80
Klee, Paul, 56, 64
knowledge systems, 83
kosmotheoros, 19

Lacan, Jacques, 27
language: acquisition of, 78, 102; compared to painting, 105, 108, 109; coincidence and, 26; and experience, 27, 101; and ideality, 90; and ideas, 31–35, 71–72; indirect, 102, 103; literary uses of, 75–77; meaning of words, 33–34, 86, 107–8; Merleau-Ponty's view of, 110–12; "natural," 74; as object and subject, 91–92, 98, 100–1; phenomenology of, 91–102; philosophy as, 28; skepticism about, 76, 89; symbolism of, 75. *See also* speech
Laplace, Pierre-Simon, and Laplacean view, 44–45, 46
Lefort, Claude, 1, 2, 3–4, 5, 102
logos, 72
Lorenz, Konrad, 49

Malraux, André, 104
Marx, Karl, and Marxist thought, 38
Matisse, Henri, 56, 64–65, 103
Mead, George Herbert, 110
Merleau-Ponty, Maurice, works by: "Eye and Mind," 4, 5, 55, 56–68; lecture notes, see *Themes from the Lectures,* below; *L'Homme transcendental,* 1; on Husserlian themes, 85–89; "Indirect Language and the Voices of Silence," 22, 55, 90, 102, 108, 109; "On the Phenomenology of Language," 5, 55, 90, 103, 108, 109; *Phenomenology of Perception,* 14, 77, 102, 109; *The Primacy of Perception,* 5; *The Prose of the World,* 3, 4, 5, 102; *Signs,* 5, 90, 102; *The Structure of Behavior,* 52; *Themes from the Lectures,* 3, 4, 55, 89, 101, 102, 109; *The Visible and the Invisible,* 4, (main themes) 9–28, (suggested additions) 5–6, (working notes) 2–3, 71
metaphysics, 56
Meyer, F., 51
Michelet, Jules, 78

modernism, 45, 66, 68, 100, 108, 109; modern painting, 56, 63–66
multiculturalism, 92

nature, 20–21; concepts of, 38–46, 47–50; humanism and, 40; and perception, 39; philosophy of, 38–44, 88; science and, 44–46
nihilism, 11
noesis and *noema,* 14

"objective activity," 38
Oedipal conflict, 82
O'Neill, John, 80
ontology: classical, 4–5, 48, 49, 50, 56, 61; Descartes's (Western), 4, 39–40, 47, 56, 59; of the flesh, 42, 53; indirect, 102; new kind of (nondualistic), 36, 50, 51, 52; phenomenology as fundamental, 83
painting, 103, 105, 106, 108, 109; Descartes's theory of vision and, 59–62, 65, 66; language compared to, 105, 108, 109; modern, 56, 63–66; painter's style, 22–23, 104; perception and, 57–59, 104; Renaissance, 56, 61, 65
passivity, 83–85
perception, 15–16, 17, 18, 21; embodied, 25, 42, 46, 57, 110; as gesture, 34; and language/speech, 22, 33, 72, 86; nature and, 39; in painting, 57–59, 104; paradox of, 16, 29; patterns of, *see* gestalts, perceptual; science and, 45; skepticism and, 10; structure of, described, 72–75; symbolism of, 75
perceptual faith, 10, 11, 12, 13
phenomenology, 90; and evolutionary theory, 52; existential, 35, 36, 98, 100, 102; as fundamental ontology, 83; of language/speech, 91–102; and philosophy, 96–102
philosophy: Being as theme of, 9, 11; of chiasm, 104; of consciousness, 80; of the flesh, 85, 88; as language, 28; Merleau-Ponty's, 36–37, 43–44, 52, 85, 88–89, 104, 110–12; of nature, 38–44, 88; phenomenological, consequences for, 96–102; rationalist (Cartesian), 62; of reflection, 16, 41; "semantic," 26; of speech, 97; "of structure," 51
Plato, 24
positivism, 28, 47
postmodernism, 45, 63, 66, 100, 107, 108, 109–10
pragmatism, 110
praxis, 74–75, 97
Proust, Marcel, 33, 79–80

rationalism, 62, 77, 83, 109, 110
reflection, 13–15; philosophies of, 16, 41
reflexivity, 31, 33–34
Renaissance painting, 56, 61, 65
reversibility, 57–58, 59, 98, 103, 106–7, 108; "nonreciprocal," 73, 75, 80, 89, 90, 109
Rilke, Rainer Maria, 66
Rodin, Auguste, 66
Rorty, Richard, 110
Russell, E. S., 49

Sartre, Jean-Paul, 56, 111
Saussure, Ferdinand de, 77–78, 79, 91, 94, 107, 108; inconsistency of, 100; theory summarized, 102
Schelling, Friedrich, 40–41
science: and Cartesian thought, 62; criticism of, 12, 44, 56–57; and new conception of nature, 44–46
sedimentation, 95, 99
"semantic philosophies," 26
signification and sign, 77–78, 89, 94–96, 110
skepticism: analysis of, 10–11; about language, 76, 89
"social fact," 111
space, 45, 61, 62; representation of, in painting, 103–4
"species slippage," 50
speech, 21–22, 23, 89–90, 93, 101; and Being, 26; bodily gestures as form of, *see* gestures; experience and, 86–87; ideality and, 88; perception and, 22, 33, 72; the problem of, 77–80. *See also* language
Stendhal (Marie Henri Beyle), 77
symbolism, 50, 55, 75, 89

Temps Moderne, Les (periodical), 5

"there exists," 9, 35, 57
time/temporality, 45–46, 80–81, 84–87, 92, 100, 105
transcendence, 24, 82
truth, 99, 110; disclosure theory of, 15

unconscious, the, 54–55

Valéry, Paul, 76
visibility, 31
vision, 63; Descartes's theory of, 59–62, 65, 66; "visual quale," 66–67. *See also* perception
von Uexull, J., 49

wave mechanics, 44